GAVIN
MULHOLLAND

FOUR SHADES OF BLACK

**THE TRADITIONAL PATH
TO BUILDING
THE COMPLETE
FIGHTER**

To Alan,
We've both come a long way no?
All the best

Important Note

The author, publishers and distributors of this book do not accept any responsibility for any loss, injury or damage caused by the use or misuse of any information or techniques described in this book. Nor do they accept any responsibility for any prosecutions or proceedings brought or instituted against any person or body as a result of the use or misuse of information or techniques described in this book or any loss, injury or damage caused thereby. The techniques and training methods described in this book require high levels of physical fitness and skill and must only be practised by those in good health whilst under qualified supervision.

Summersdale Publishers Ltd
46 West Street
Chichester
West Sussex
PO19 1RP
UK

www.summersdale.com

Printed and bound in Belgium

ISBN: 1-8402-4650-2

ISBN13: 978-1-8402-4650-6

Contents

PREFACE

When I first started to explore the martial arts for a practical solution to my fear of violent confrontation, I came upon many systems that purported to offer a comprehensive solution. None of them did. A few offered limitation, a lot offered sport (dressed up as combat), and most offered a poor imitation. None that I could find offered an honest, in-your-face, blood-and-snot system for surviving a violent encounter.

The art I studied longest, and the one that came closest to fulfilling its promise of being a *martial* system, was Karate. Of all the arts I studied — and there were many — this was the most comprehensive. There was only one problem. The art that I was learning did not teach its full curriculum. There was a plethora of techniques stored in the kata that was largely ignored. I was only taught a *synopsis* of Karate, a long-range standing art that did not address many vital areas, not least standing and ground-grappling.

I found this confusing. I could see with my own eyes that the kata contained techniques from just about any and every range — Judo, Thai boxing, wrestling, Western boxing, weapons — but these were not taught in class. Or if they were, they were relegated to a few repetitions of the bunkai that offered an appetiser, but not a competence.

That's why I decided to spend some serious mat time in all the arts — Judo and Western boxing to name but two — that might fill the gap left by my previous training. My sojourn left me both intrigued and annoyed.

Intriguing was the fact that everything I learned in these other arts I recognised and traced back to my original system of Karate. All of it. It was all in the kata.

Annoying was the attitude of many of my contemporaries (at the time). Like jealous husbands they accused me of infidelity with other arts; they said I had abandoned my art, not realising that what I had discovered *was* traditional Karate (as opposed to a Karate dilute). I felt alone in my belief that Karate taught real could be all-encompassing if you were brave enough not to take 'yes' for an answer.

That is until I started to read great books by the likes of Iain Abernethy and more recently this amazing book by Gavin Mulholland. Not only has Gavin discovered and expanded on all of these points, he has also identified, in the layout of the Goju kata, an actual progressive order of combat; avoidance, pre-emptive blitzing, trapping and ripping, tachi waza and ne waza.

I can't tell you how exciting it is for me to find such a like-minded soul, someone else who is speaking the same language. That is why I highly recommend this authentic book, its contents and its author.

It is very easy in the wake of UFC (Ultimate Fighting Championship) and Vale Tudo to slate Karate as an old-fashioned art with gaping limitations. Many of the uninitiated, looking for the latest zeitgeist, have been guilty of this, tilting their lance at something (anything) they know little about. But when I see the brave warriors that step into the cage or the UFC, I don't see a different art to the one that Gavin writes so eloquently about, I do not see an art that is any better or any worse than Karate, I actually see the Karate schematic, laid out and manifest, how it should look if it is taught properly.

Karate was developed in times of war, and the masters of old were not remiss when they catalogued their findings. The genius that they left is complete, an empirical legacy for the contemporary masters to rediscover — those brave enough or insightful enough to leave the trunk of the tree and explore some of its many branches.

Gavin is one such master and I implore everyone who is 'searching' to read this book — it is both valuable and long overdue.

Geoff Thompson. BAFTA-winning Writer,
Teacher, Martial Artist

A thorough understanding of kata is vital if you wish to practise Karate as a holistic and pragmatic fighting system. The great tragedy is that very few people understand the true nature of kata and hence it is rarely taught correctly. Kata is widely thought to be nothing more than an antiquated aesthetic dance that has no relation to combat. To be clear, when kata is approached incorrectly it is quite true to say it has no relation to combat. However, the fault does not lie

agreement. Indeed many of those present commented on how our sections dovetailed seamlessly: it was almost as if we'd planned it!

It's always good to meet someone who holds similar views on the martial arts so when Gavin mentioned he'd been planning this book I was excited. There are only a small number of good books on kata application so I knew it would be in great demand and

FOREWORD

with kata itself, but in the fact that it has been taught incorrectly. An even bigger problem facing modern karateka is that there are comparatively few people who understand kata correctly and can provide instruction in what is the very essence of Karate. Thankfully there are people like Gavin Mulholland — and books like this one.

Both Gavin and I are known for our pragmatic approach to Karate and therefore a seminar with us both was organised under the banner of 'Karate: The Practical Fighting Art'. We'd never taught together before and had no way of knowing if our approaches were compatible. In the run-up, we chatted a few times on the phone but never discussed any detail; the one thing we did decide was that Gavin would teach the first hour on the practical use of stances. The seminar was very well attended and after the warm-up Gavin opened with the line, 'The two most misunderstood words in Karate are "stance" and "block".' At that point I knew we had very similar views on Karate. Although we practise differing styles, when it came down to core principle and concepts we found ourselves in perfect

warmly welcomed by the growing number of karateka who wish to understand kata and practise their art as the practical fighting system it was intended to be. When he asked if I'd like to contribute a foreword I was honoured, and having read numerous articles by Gavin in the UK martial arts press, I was expecting something special. I was not disappointed! This book should be in the library of all serious karateka.

This great book explains in a direct and uncomplicated way how kata is central to Karate. Although the book concentrates on the Goju kata, the central message is much wider and the lessons apply to students of all styles. Kata are the very essence of Karate and so much more than a haphazard collection of techniques. Kata were created to record the key principles of the various Karate systems and to guide the karateka's study. They don't record every single technique, but they do record the key principles upon which the techniques are based and which are central to the fighting system recorded. These key principles, and the numerous ways in which they can be applied, should be at the centre of Karate study.

An analogy I've found useful to explain how kata records the essence of Karate is to think of Karate as being like an oak tree. An oak tree is vast, both in terms of its size and years lived, but everything about that tree, and everything required to reproduce it, is found in a single acorn. The various Karate styles produce kata in the same way that an oak tree produces acorns. Both the acorn and the kata are not as vast as the thing that created them, but they record them perfectly. For an acorn to become an oak tree it must be correctly planted and nurtured. For a kata to become a fighting system it must be correctly studied and practised. It is here that we find one of modern Karate's biggest failings, in that the kata are rarely studied. To return to my analogy, we have the seeds but we don't plant them.

In this book Gavin explains how the four kata learnt up to black belt within the Goju Ryu system represent the fields of study that the karateka should undertake as they progress. Gekisai-Dai-Ichi will guide the karateka's study of hard 'attack and smash' techniques. Gekisai-Dai-Ni furthers the student's understanding of attack and smash by tightening the range and introducing methods of unbalancing and redirection. Once the student understands these lessons they move on to Saifa, which guides the student's study of grabbing, locking and disengaging. The final kata of the four is Seiunchin which guides the student through their study of sticking, grappling and close-quarter combat. Gavin shows how the four kata constitute a logical and coherent guide to the techniques and principles that will make the karateka a complete fighter.

This combative progression is the key to understanding these four kata and indeed the system of Goju Ryu Karate itself, but students of other styles should understand that this type of combative progression can be found within their own kata and should be central to their own training.

The Pinan/Heian kata of Wado Ryu, Shito Ryu and Shotokan also adhere to a combative progression: the first three kata dealing with the basics of the first three stages of the fight (the initial exchange of limbs, the establishing of a datum/grip and counters to such techniques, and finally grappling and fighting from a clinch). The last two kata of the Pinan/Heian kata build upon the basic concepts introduced by the first three and move on to include combining the various methods and the transitions between ranges. Indeed, individual kata such as Kushanku — the kata being a record of the teachings of a Chinese martial artist by the same name — are also based on a combative progression: the early techniques introduce the basics and the later techniques represent the more advanced aspects of Kushanku's teaching.

Regardless of style, all karateka should read and digest the information contained within this excellent book. There can be few people more qualified to write a book such as this. Gavin Mulholland is someone who fully understands the realities of combat and kata and if you wish to practise Karate as the pragmatic fighting system it was intended to be, you should familiarise yourself with Gavin's work. This is a thorough and accessible explanation of everything you need to know to make sense of kata and become a complete fighter. *Four Shades of Black* is a must-read book that is certain to become a modern classic.

Enjoy!

Iain Abernethy. Author of Bunkai-Jutsu:
*The Practical Application
of Karate Kata.*

INTRODUCTION

Long before their arrival on our shores in the late nineteenth century, the martial arts had already achieved the status of myth and legend. Sailors, soldiers and adventurers returning from the East told fantastic stories of exotic places inhabited by indestructible fighting men — men able to take on, and defeat, whole armies with their bare hands.

While there were always those who had followed the path of the martial arts, it was ultimately the defeat of imperial Japan and the end of the Second World War that unleashed what we would now call 'mainstream martial arts' into the consciousness of everyday people.

Since that time, every decade appears to have had its favourite style as people have struggled to find this art of legend so firmly ingrained in the psyche of those drawn to the martial arts. First there was Ju-jitsu. In the 1960s it was Judo. The 1970s saw Karate come to the fore closely followed by Kung Fu. Kick-boxing ruled the 1980s and the 1990s saw the revolution that is now known as MMA (Mixed Martial Arts) explode onto the scene in the form of the Ultimate Fighting Championship (UFC).

It seems as if, like the seven-year itch, people are only prepared to give a system so long to prove itself. Then it's off with the heavy, unbleached gi, on with the light, pure white one. Off with the gi altogether, on with the spangly star-studded silk trousers. Off with the spangly trousers and on with the tight Lycra pants; and on it goes.

The problem is really two-fold: firstly, people are still seeking the myth which in our time has been perpetuated and magnified by popular TV and films; and secondly, eight to ten years is simply not enough time to achieve anything close to perfection. As the old masters have been telling us all along, the study of a martial art is a lifelong endeavour.

But how can that be? If you take Karate for example, how can you study something as simple as punching and kicking for a lifetime and furthermore, why would you want to?

The answer is simple. You can't, you wouldn't, and here's the crux of the matter, you were never supposed to. Karate in its original form was a complete fighting system — stand-up, ground-fighting, headbutts, bites, rips, gouges, long-range, close-quarter — all in, the lot.

But how could I possibly know that? Especially when so many people would disagree with me? Again, the answer is simple. I know because the founders told me. I know that Okinawan Goju Ryu contains all of these things because Chojun Miyagi Sensei told me so. What's more, he not only told me they exist, he showed me where to find them, when to train in each, and how to train in each area of combat most effectively. In fact, he told me how to do it all.

And how did he do this? He did it through the real legacy of genius that he left us. He did it through the DVD of his day. He recorded the various areas of required study and he outlined roughly how long we should be training in each. He pointed the way and gave a few examples of the sorts of things we should be looking at.

… he did it through kata.

You will often hear martial artists refer to a student's progression in the martial arts as following the *'Way'* or the *'Path'*.

A few have taken this to mean that there is only one way – their way, of course. Others have taken it to mean that martial arts have to become your 'way of life' – infusing and permeating every element of your daily life, from your job to your personal relationships, to doing the dishes.

However, to many of us, the whole concept of a 'way' or a 'path' signifies a journey of some sort – movement and progression across a territory, previously explored and hopefully recorded. This is further backed up in the language of the Japanese martial arts where 'teacher' (Sensei) literally translates as *'one who has gone before'*.

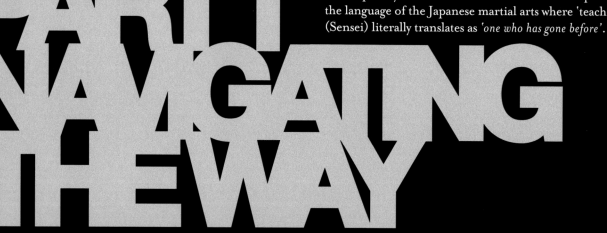

PART 1
NAVIGATING THE WAY

'The Way is in training.' Miyamoto Musashi

In this sense, we are all on the same journey of martial knowledge and self-discovery. From the most recent convert to the most grizzled of old sweats, we tread the same path, we seek the same goals, and we supposedly navigate our way across the same territory.

But how do we do that? How can we possibly navigate our way around something as vast as the martial arts without straying from the path, ending up down a blind alley, or just simply getting lost? That's easy. Ask any expert in orienteering or navigation, military or civilian, and they will tell you that to navigate successfully you basically need just two things – you need a map, and you need a compass.

Well, guess what? We've got them both.

'*Gu ming si yi — By the name of a thing,
one is reminded of its function*'
Chinese saying

CHAPTER 1
THE MAP

'*So, what's all this kata stuff about then?*' Of all the deep, probing, awkward and downright bizarre questions that you regularly get asked in the martial arts, this has got to be the one which every one of us dreads. In over thirty years of martial arts training I don't think I have heard this particular question answered in the same way twice — ever. A quick trawl of the internet reveals the extent of the confusion:

> *Formal, prearranged exercise*
> *A 'form' or prescribed pattern of movement*
> *The set techniques in a martial art*
> *A manner of movement and pose proper to a style*
> *Predetermined sequences of movements used as a learning tool*
> *Stylised set of movements that use a variety of blocks and strikes against an invisible opponent*
> *Formal exercises that comprise a series of grappling or striking movements that imitate fighting situations*

So, to sum up, descriptions range from imitating fighting situations, to attacking an invisible opponent, to a list of techniques, to moving in a way deemed 'proper' to a style, to a simple type of exercise. Clearly no real consensus there then.

Furthermore, if any of these descriptions did represent what kata was all about, why would we need so many of them? Something just doesn't add up.

Despite what some people think these days, the kata do not hold the entirety of any given system — nor were they ever intended to. There have always been elements of Karate which sit outside the kata in terms of their core learning. Often they are alluded to in the kata, but the actual study of them is expected to be done elsewhere — grappling and weaponry to name just two.

In the days of 'Te' and 'Tode' (Okinawa's precursors to Karate), grappling and weaponry were very much a part of the early systems — long before the name 'Karate' came about, that is. The name 'Karate' only came into being in Okinawa on 25 October 1936 when the then masters of the native systems of 'Te' met to discuss how the Okinawan martial arts might best be moved forward into a new era. At that meeting it was agreed that the combat systems they were currently practising should come together under the umbrella name of Kara-Te — 'empty hand'.

Many people continue to read very deeply into the noble naming of this ancient art, completely ignoring the fact that a large part of its origin was simple, straightforward xenophobia — the old names sounded too Chinese. In fact, one particularly well known master went so far as to say that the continued use of the 'China' character (as in 'China Hand' — Tode) was both *'inappropriate'* and *'degrading'*. For political and cultural reasons, the old names needed to be replaced with something more 'Japanese'.

This is not unique in the martial arts and similar things can be seen in the naming of Taekwondo, a Korean art actually founded on Japanese Karate but again politically reluctant to say so. And again in Yung Hi Choi (Choi Baedal) changing his name to sound more Japanese and less Korean. Choi of course went on to become the legendary Kyokushinkai founder, Masutatsu Oyama. The fact that Oyama was actually Korean is still denied in some circles in Japan today but he remains something of a national hero in Korea itself. If you ever watch the South Korean film on Mas Oyama's life, *Fighter in the Wind*, you will find not one single mention of Oyama's Japanese Karate instructors, Gogen Yamaguchi (Goju Kai) and Gichin Funakoshi (Shotokan). All you see is a Korean fighter taking on and beating all the best fighters in Japan. Clearly this is still a popular political message and so it seems some things never change.

Furthermore, the name 'empty hand' has led many to ignore the old association of Kobudo weaponry with old Karate and assume that 'empty hand' must mean no weapons.

Similarly, because it is much harder to represent a grappling technique with the absence of a partner than it is to represent a striking one, many people have reached the mistaken conclusion that Karate contains no grappling — possibly the single greatest error and disservice ever done to the complete fighting art of Okinawan Karate. Talk about defanging the snake.

The kata do allude to grappling techniques, as they allude to all areas of study, and this is the key. The individual kata are pointing you in the direction of your next area of study.

It's not about patterns of movement, it's not about balance and coordination, it's not about 22 new techniques (although all those do come with the package); it is about telling you what to investigate, study and practise next.

This is why people used to spend years on a single kata. This is why your Sensei gets annoyed to see you practising a kata three levels above your grade. And this is where all the bits and pieces that you know, but cannot find in a specific kata, belong. And it is all revealed in the naming of the kata.

If we take Okinawan Goju Ryu as an example, we can see that the kata have not just been put together willy-nilly, but that each clearly alludes to a specific area of progressive study.

Goju translates as hard/soft and one of the basic principles of the style is that you start off hard (Go) and increasingly progress towards a more subtle and skilful soft (Ju) technique. The first Goju kata is called Gekisai-Dai-Ichi which translates as *'Attack and*

Smash Number One'. The 'essence' of this kata is right there for all to see in the title itself. Gekisai-Dai-Ichi is the start point and it is telling you to study and investigate hard-style attack-and-smash techniques.

This is done in much the same way as a university lecture. The lecture itself does not tell you what you need to know — it tells you the 'area' that you need to be researching for yourself. This is why the old arguments of high or low kicks not existing in the kata are entirely irrelevant. At this stage of your training you are practising and developing the basic ability of an all-out attack-and-smash type defence. For many years Karate practitioners have agonised over the lack of high kicks in the kata. However, while you can perform a reasonable front-kick into open air it is all but impossible to do the same with a round-kick. An effective high or low round-kick involves you 'losing' your balance momentarily (like walking) and it is the impact of the kick that sets you right again. To perform a round-kick with no impact you must modify it substantially to enable you to kick while staying 'on balance'. That's why these kicks are not overtly demonstrated within the kata. And they don't need to be — what does it matter if I smash someone with a front-kick or a round-kick? It doesn't; it is the mindset and the area of combat that is important.

In Gekisai-Dai-Ichi, almost all the techniques are long range and closed fist. This means that at this stage the fight is at a distance. Somewhat unrealistic in actual combat perhaps, but it is the easiest to learn and definitely the place to start.

After six months or so, the new student moves on to Gekisai-Dai-Ni — 'Attack and Smash Number Two'. Now, on the surface this is a very similar kata to the first one with the addition of more open handed techniques. In fact, it is so similar that it has led many to question the need for two kata that look so similar. To this end some schools have (mistakenly, in my

opinion) dropped one or other of the Gekisai kata from their system.

However, when you begin to look at the kata of your ryu as a system of progressive learning rather than as a patchwork of different kata, the picture starts to become clear. The difference between Gekisai-Dai-Ichi and Gekisai-Dai-Ni is not in movement, but in range. The open-hand techniques of the second kata tell you that the range has been closed somewhat and now you are using sukami hike, pull/push, unbalancing and redirection techniques and strategies before 'smashing' your opponent. This is a much higher level of skill than the simple attack-and-smash of Gekisai-Dai-Ichi.

The next kata in the Goju syllabus is Saifa, which roughly translates as 'Tearing' (more accurately 'Smash and Tear' but it is the tearing element that gives us the next clue). By this stage the student has been training for about one year and their focus has been on relatively hard, stand-up fighting techniques. Over the course of that year the focus has shifted from simple move-block-hit (Gekisai-Dai-Ichi) to a more skilful move-redirect-unbalance-hit (Gekisai-Dai-Ni). It is now time to close the area of combat still further.

The 'tearing' in Saifa alludes to the fact that the area of attack has now closed to the point where your attacker has actually grabbed you. This is confirmed in the first three movements of the kata where three basic principles of disengaging from a grab are shown. Notice that I say 'principles', not 'techniques'. The techniques will vary, the principles will not. In this case the basic principles are:

> To focus on the weakest part of the grabbing hand (the thumb/finger)
> To use body shift to put pressure on the wrist before attacking the weakest part of the grabbing hand
> To control the body and arm before putting pressure on the wrist and attacking the weakest part of the grabbing hand

So, for the next six months or so, you as a martial artist are expected to investigate all manner of grabs and locks and how to tear yourself away from them. Not only the grabs shown in the kata (they are just examples), but *all* grabs and holds — standing and on the ground. It is your next level of understanding and your focused area of study — for now. Notice that an element of 'smash' still remains at this stage. This is more about getting clear of an attacker than it is about staying there and controlling them. That comes next.

And where it appears is in the next kata: Seiunchin — *'Trapping Battle'*.

Trapping battle, as the name implies, is basically a grappling kata that stresses muchimi (sticking) and close-quarter fighting. During the kata, students should concentrate on the muscles and structures that generate the techniques and postures, rather than simply the techniques and postures themselves.

The student is probably about brown belt level by now and the fight has closed to the much more realistic range of close-quarters. I worked on the doors of pubs and clubs around London and the UK for over 15 years and, like it or not, this is where fights take place. Not necessarily, as some claim, on the ground (more about that later), but definitely up-close and dirty.

Seiunchin is your indicator that it is time to study grappling and close-quarter combat in all its many shapes and forms — stand-up, on the ground, throws, counters, take-downs, preventing others from taking you down, etc, etc.

Once you start to look for meaning in the names and sequence of the kata you can begin to see why the founders structured the 'programme' in the way they did. It is not simply a matter of taking a couple of kata from Goju, a couple from Wado and a couple you make up yourself and piecing them together

to form some new 'style'. What you have is a deeply logical and practical guide as to how to structure your training — *for years to come.*

From a Goju perspective you will start by working on hard basic attacks, aiming simply to smash your way through an attacker. Effective yes, but it is pretty basic and, to a certain extent, it does take youth and strength. The next stage is to do the same but with more skill, movement and subtle redirection. Then as the area of combat continues to close, you need to train to disengage from grabs and holds to get back to the attack-and-smash fighting range you are already comfortable with. Finally, we reach full-on close-quarter combat and we are expected to train to deal with it. Not just escaping from grabs and holds but using them ourselves to control and defeat our opponents.

If you have ever worked in a nightclub, or even gone to one for that matter, you will see that it is always the young, inexperienced door guys who are punching people out. The old sweats just tie aggressive punters up in knots and chuck them out. You will notice that it is the old boys who are not actually hurting anybody. This is a far higher level of skill and it takes time and it takes experience to achieve.

The gift of our founders is that they have 'gone before' and have presented us with a unique and usable training map in order to do just that — learn to defend yourself straight away, but then progress both physically and spiritually to the point where, in a conflict, you are not only able to protect yourself, but to protect your attacker as well. These are the highest goals of the martial arts and the way to achieve them has been with us all along — in the progressive programme of kata laid out by the founders all those years ago.

*'A rusty nail placed near a faithful compass,
will sway it from the truth'*
Walter Scott

CHAPTER 2
THE COMPASS

So, we have the map. It was in front of us all along. We have a clearly laid-out guide indicating what area of combat to train in and for how long before gradually decreasing the range and increasing the pressure as we progress towards our complete, rounded, martial artist goal.

But the map on its own isn't enough. Remember, in order to navigate competently, we need two things — we need a map, and we need a compass. So we have the map — where is the compass?

Well, once again, it's right in front of us. What do we have within the traditional martial arts that helps us find a direction, plot a course, and measure our progression along that course? What do we have that allows us to triangulate our position in reference to ourselves, our peers and those who have gone before?

We have the grading system. We have our compass.

The use of the grading system and its coloured belts is one of the most contentious issues within traditional Karate today, and certainly one of the most talked about. The current tide of thinking seems to have moved against it with the suggestion that it is just *rewards for the children*. I'd like to put some of that straight.

The grading system used in Karate today was actually the brainchild of the brilliant and innovative founder of Judo, Dr Jigoro Kano. Dr Kano was something of a visionary and created the system in the 1880s, awarding his first black sash in 1886. The sash was replaced around 1907 by the kuri obi (black belt) that we use today.

The original system had only two colours – white belts for the novice or 'unranked' students (mudansha) and black belts for the more senior or 'ranked' students (yudansha).

The term 'mudansha' is a combination of three terms: mu is a Zen term denoting 'nothingness', dan means 'rank' and sha means 'person'. It is important to understand that a state of nothingness does not hold the same negative connotations in the East as it does in the West. It simply reflects the cyclical nature of the martial path: the beginning state of nothingness also being the highest attainable state.

For senior students, *yu* is simply a possessive term so 'yudansha' literally translates as 'person possessing rank'.

The use of black and white belts therefore held much deeper symbolism than seems to be present today. At its most basic level, it is a symbolic representation of the dualistic Yin/Yang concept which is ever-present in martial philosophy.

Despite the use of a dual colour system, levels of progression still existed within the kyu ranks and eventually those who were deemed to be nearing the end of their 'novice' phase (usually around five or six years) began to wear brown belts to signify that they would soon be ranked.

Karate adopted Kano's kyu/dan ranking system in Japan around 1924 and, as with many aspects of modern Karate such as large classes, uniforms, and military-style basics, there was a reverse feedback to Okinawa from mainland Japan.

An outward representation of the levels of achievement within the kyu grade ranks was inevitable and over the next few decades various coloured belts were introduced to denote the ten novice grades leading up to black belt.

Despite the fact that there are ten novice *grades*, there are really only four *levels*. The first, and lowest, level is from white to orange belt (tenth to seventh kyu). The step up to green belt (incorporating green to purple belts – sixth to fourth kyu) represents the next level and, to many, the first sign of strength. In my own association it is at this level that students are 'badged'. The club badge cannot be bought and is an award signifying the student's graduation from basic training. The next level is the brown belt (third to first kyu) and of course, the final level sees the student entering the black belt ranks and beginning Karate proper.

It is a very recent notion to think that the colours were put in place to encourage children. The original purpose of the coloured belt system had a much higher goal indeed. In fact it symbolically and physically seeks to effect one of the most rewarding and fundamental changes that the martial arts has to offer a practitioner – the gradual transition from external goal seeker to internal seeker of truth.

It's all about the gradual transition from external to internal drives and that's why we have three brown belts on the immediate run-up to black belt.

Generally speaking, when you start out in a Karate club, there are gradings every three or four months and you get a nice new outward symbol of that achievement — a new coloured belt. Despite the fact that many people will tell you that they don't care about such rewards, nine times out of ten this is rubbish and there are plenty of psychological studies on motivation, rewards and drives to prove this beyond any reasonable doubt.

Get to green belt (sixth kyu) and the gradings drop to once every six months or so. Then you hit brown belt. In Karate terms, this is Long Drag! You have three brown belts to get through and gradings only come once a year — but they still come and some schools put black tags on their brown belts to denote the different levels in a more subtle manner than a full colour change. So now that you are no longer getting a highly visible outward incentive to carry on, the focus of your attention has to shift to the more internal goal of acquiring skill for its own sake. That's why if students get to brown belt too quickly, so many will drop out — they have simply not yet managed that shift of focus and the lack of a 'reward' for them still translates into a lack of motivation.

Then, at last, black belt.

Contrary to popular opinion, it is actually the black belt that represents 'no belt', not the white one. It is the one that is supposed to say, *'Okay guys, we're all the same now. Let's forget about the belt system and get on with it.'* That's why I personally dislike those little gold dan bars. To my mind, a high grade black belt should wear the same belt as the newest shodan because we are supposed to have dispensed with those outward signs of progression and are now both concentrating on internal development.

That's also why when someone tells me they don't believe in the grading system, I will say fine — get yourself a black belt and you can forget all about it.

The positive effects of the grading system have been proven time and time again. It's no coincidence that a lot of today's Kick-boxing classes use a coloured belt system to indicate and facilitate progression. It's no coincidence that a lot of Kung Fu schools use coloured sashes to denote progression. It's no coincidence that a number of ring-combat systems now choose to indicate a student's progress through a series of coloured gloves. And it's no coincidence that some schools of Jeet Kune Do, possibly one of traditional Karate's loudest critics, now choose to denote rank and progression through a series of coloured T-shirts.

One of the biggest misconceptions, both in and out of the martial arts fraternity, is that being a black belt represents being an expert. As many an unfortunate shodan has found out in their local pub car park, and much to the endless amusement of the general press, nothing could be further from the truth. Black belt status really only indicates a graduation to a new beginning.

All the other grades are simply 'novice' grades. Black belt is the level at which you begin to learn Karate. Have you never wondered why a first level black belt is known as a shodan and not an *Ichidan*? *Ichi* means 'one' or 'first', but *sho* means 'beginning'. Reaching this beginning level simply means you have achieved a rudimentary level of proficiency in the basics and are now ready to start learning Karate.

Despite what one might see passed off as martial arts these days, one of the prerequisites for this 'new beginning' is supposed to be the absence of ego and an internal drive towards self-improvement.

Once you realise that the grading system was put in place to try and achieve these goals, you will come to realise that failure is just as important as success, if not more so.

Students should fail gradings. We all should. It's just that not everyone has the courage to put themselves under such harsh scrutiny. As we used to understand before words like 'success' and 'failure' were deemed to be too judgemental, the real development of the self ('character' as it used to be known) comes from failure. Success is all well and good in its place, but the lessons of picking yourself up and carrying on after a setback represent some of the truly developmental moments in your life.

Why do you think your granny was the toughest person you ever met? It's because times really did used to be tough and she had been knocked down more times than she would ever say — but she got up, and she got up, and she kept on getting up until it became so ingrained in her that it was simply what she did — she took a knock, shook it off, and carried on.

The dojo is a little microcosm of the 'real' world. It is a 'safe' environment in which people can seek enlightenment and grow spiritually through engaging in combat and facing their fears. If you are not failing your students during gradings you are doing them a massive disservice. I don't think I know of any great martial artists, or great anyone for that matter, who didn't get there via a series of failures, knocks and setbacks. Well, guess what? It was those very failures, knocks and setbacks that ultimately led them to greatness.

Dealing with success is easy. Dealing with failure takes courage, tenacity and a massive amount of humility. The martial arts have long claimed to gift these traits to their practitioners but so often they appear to be in scant supply. 'Courage' seems to equate to entering a semi-contact tournament (if you're feeling all right that day, and it's not too far away). 'Tenacity' is demonstrated by turning up for training twice a week. And 'humility' is limited to the *'It's okay, you don't need to call me Soke — Grandmaster will do just fine'* brigade. None of this would happen if people failed more gradings and learned the real lessons available through the grading system.

To build genuine courage, tenacity and humility alongside the absence of ego and an internal drive towards self-improvement takes time. And correct management of the grading system with its highs and lows, passes and fails, increasing time between external rewards, and decreasing contrast between those rewards, is a fantastic tool for achieving those goals.

In short, the grading system is our compass and it helps to guide us in our first tentative steps into the unknown territory of the arts. It helps to illuminate our chosen path, and it allows us to plot a course for our future training and development. However, used correctly it will do far more than that. The grading system can help facilitate one of the most rewarding and fundamental of changes possible through the martial arts — the shift from external goal seeker to internal seeker of truth. In fact, the transition from being a kyu grade to being a dan grade.

PART 2
FUNDAMENTALS

It was never the intention of this book to cover basic
Karate techniques. In fact, some general assumptions
have been made as to the reader's efficiency in
basic technique, or, at the very least, their access to
reasonable instruction in those methods. However,
principles and strategies underlying the correct use
of what we commonly refer to as 'basics' are anything
but basic.

CHAPTER 3
PUNCHES

I remember the day well — and so will you. Throughout your martial arts career, it is possible to identify seminal moments when something clicks; some basic truth bubbles to the surface, something that you half-knew already suddenly comes into sharp focus. And from that moment everything changes — nothing is ever quite the same again.

For me, one such moment happened in the winter of 1986 while training under the Goju master Kyoshi Kim Roberts. Kyoshi was talking about power generation and lamenting the fact that many karateka of the day (and still today, if the truth be told) had failed to recognise the full diversity and range of punching and punches within their own kata and systems. He went on to show jabs (kazami tsuki), crosses (kosa tsuki), hooks (kagi tsuki) and uppercuts (age tsuki), every one of them taken directly from the kata, and it suddenly and shockingly dawned on me — there was no such thing as a 'Karate punch'.

The 'traditional' fist at shoulder height with the other fist chambered high to the side of the chest in Goju (low by the hip for Shotokan and Wado) was and remains a simple training device. It was never intended to represent the *only* punch to be used in Karate. However, what this standard 'Karate punch' does is teach some fundamental truths about power generation and punching in general.

In order to see how it does this, it is important to understand that the system you practise is supposed to be working as a whole. You are not learning a wide variety of disparate and unrelated bits and pieces — you are learning a series of specific elements which when put together will produce the fighter and the martial artist. In the case of punching, the 'Karate punch' only teaches part of the story, but it does it brilliantly.

In essence a punch has three phases: the 'trigger', when the punch is initially fired; the release, where the punch flies freely to its target; and, of course, the impact, where the fist strikes the target. The standard Karate line-up punch delivered into thin air only teaches the initial phase; the trigger.

It goes without saying that this method of punching can never teach you anything about impact; that's where makiwara, pads and kumite come into play. Neither can it teach anything about the free flight to target. In order to impact with maximum force, a punch must *accelerate* all the way into the target. In order to do this all tension needs to be taken out of the punching limb immediately after the punch is fired. Psychologically this can only be done if you know that there is something there to hit which will arrest your movement. When punching into thin air, you subconsciously (but necessarily) *decelerate* your punch, almost from the point of the trigger. To do anything else would lead to jarring of the elbow joint and that common problem, tennis elbow.

So why in Karate do we focus so heavily on the initial trigger phase? Well again, it all makes perfect sense. The initial explosion of a punch is the single most important element in generating power, but it needs drilling. Get this right and once you start hitting something heavy, the rest will simply fall into place.

So, how does it work? If you watch a baseball player, a cricketer or a golfer hit a ball, you will notice they generate a huge amount of torque by twisting their body towards the target while the bat or club lags behind before accelerating massively in order to catch up with the rest of the body. It is this torque that fires the trigger and that generates the massive amount of power that enables someone like Tiger Woods to hit a golf ball over 400 yards when someone twice his size would struggle to hit it 200.

When you punch in a line-up your attention should really be on the chambered hand not, as most people seem to do, on the extended fist. If you are punching to a count, the initial movement should be a slight backward movement of the punching hand while the hip on the punching side should move slightly forward. This generates the torque which creates a tension diagonally across your body and engages the stretch reflex across your shoulder/chest which will fire that punch out like a bullet.

Once you realise this you will see that *all* punches use this stretch reflex to generate power — reverse punches, crosses, hooks, uppercuts; all of them. The main difference is that in application you rarely draw the striking hand back; rather you throw your body forward leaving the shoulder to lag behind to create the stretch, tension and torque you need to really explode that punch forward. Watch some of Mike Tyson's early knockouts and you will see this 'Karate punch' in all its intended glory.

In the early stages of Karate training the primary place we learn these lessons is the line-up and, drilled constantly, this is a fantastic tool for developing power. However, if you stop between your punches and/or your initial movement is simply a push forward, these invaluable lessons will be lost.

Of course, in order to develop a truly powerful punch you must now transfer these lessons onto a makiwara/bag/person in order to work the other two elements (flight and impact). Alongside relaxation, this is really the secret of powerful punching and the mechanism for developing such power has always existed in codified form, within what has rather annoyingly become known as the 'Karate punch'.

CHAPTER 4
KICKS

While we all accept that kicking forms an integral part of our Karate systems, there is ongoing discussion regarding the validity, usefulness and effectiveness of kicking high to the head. Having spent many years involved in conflict and confrontation resolution, I share the concerns raised by the prospect of attempting high kicks in a real situation. Nevertheless, I also believe that many have used these concerns as an excuse not to train in what I have come to see as an important aspect of combat training.

Goju Ryu is often referred to as a close-quarter fighting system and this in itself would appear to indicate a limited need for high kicks. Furthermore, the vast majority of people involved in security will tell you that the use of high kicks in an actual confrontation is ill-advised at best, dangerous (to the kicker) at worst. Finally, high kicks do not appear to feature very heavily, if at all, in any of the early kata.

These three basic facts in themselves raise some serious questions about kicking, kicks, and their role in combat and combat training. And the main question has to be, should we be training in high kicks at all? And the answer is a resounding yes, we should.

Despite my own research, findings and beliefs, it is not my intention to try to convince people that high kicks have always existed in Karate. However, the basic truth is that despite what you may believe historically, they exist now and as such, we need to understand how to deal with them.

It is a sad truth that many kids these days learn their 'fighting skills' from the television. They see some cool stuff and they want to do it — and that includes high kicks. It is as much a fallacy to believe that this form of attack does not exist on the street as it was to believe that no one performed a knife attack in that overhead Psycho-type manner.

As it happens a lot of knife attacks are actually domestic in nature and guess where the disgruntled wife learnt her knife skills? Correct, television. They may not be the most sophisticated of strategies but overhead knife attacks do exist in the outside world and so do high kicks.

On top of that there are martial artists/doormen out there who are very versed in the language of confrontation and conflict who can (and do) knock people out with kicks — Nick Hughes and Terry O'Neil to name two of the better known. Both of these men (and a great many more) will testify to the benefits of having such a weapon in your arsenal. Furthermore, despite shaky beginnings, the high kick has not been without its successes in the Octagon of the UFC. High kicks are indeed risky, but there are still people out there who can use them to devastating effect.

No matter what style you practise, if it is your intention to move the fight into close-quarters you will need to pass through a range where a good kicker could cause you serious trouble. If no one in your dojo is able to perform high kicks, then how will students gain the experience needed in order to deal with such an attack should the need arise?

As for high kicks not existing in kata, we will see later in the book that they are alluded to and indeed always have been. It is easy enough to perform a front kick into thin air without overly compromising the structure and integrity of the kick. The same cannot be said of a high round kick. People talk about 'balance' in regard to kicking but the truth is that we are not referring to being in *balance*, rather we are referring to being in *control* of your balance and that involves losing it. Balance must be lost in order to transfer all of that rotational power into the kick and ultimately into your opponent. To perform the same kick into thin air requires such fundamental alterations as to almost change the

nature and structure of the kick in its entirety. In short, in order to perform a high round kick into thin air you must by definition kick incorrectly. And the kata were not put together to teach people to perform techniques incorrectly.

Rather, high kicks, side kicks, high round kicks, low round kicks — in fact all manner of kicks are referred to and alluded to in the spirit of the individual kata themselves. For example, as we have seen, the first Gekisai kata in Goju translates as 'attack and smash' and it is the concept of attacking and smashing that is important, not just the front-kick example demonstrated in the kata itself. You will smash an attacker through whatever openings he leaves, and you will smash him with whatever tool is best for the job in that instant. Sometimes that will be a front-kick, sometimes a thigh kick, sometimes it will be a high round kick, and it's all Karate.

The study of any martial art is a lifelong endeavour and there will inevitably come a time in your Karate when high kicks are no longer a viable option for you, but that time should not be when you are 22 years old. Like it or not, kicking is a fundamental expression of Karate and you need to be familiar and competent with all manner of kicks and kicking styles, not only to be able to use them yourself but, more importantly, to be able to defend against them should the need arise.

CHAPTER 5
BLOCKS

One particular area of Karate training that has been systematically misinterpreted, over-stylised and misunderstood over the years is the area of 'blocking'. In fact, blocking has become so limited in the way it is taught and trained today that it has even been labelled 'irrelevant' by some other styles and combat sports.

Other fight-based disciplines such as boxing, or MMA, spend a much higher proportion of their training time with somebody *actually* trying to hit them, and yet, seemingly perversely, they appear to spend little if any time at all practising that mainstay of Karate training — blocking.

How can that be? It is my contention that we in the Karate fraternity have lost our way somewhat with regard to the study and use of blocks. In order to begin to understand where we might have started to stray from the path, let's turn to the dictionary to see what it means to 'block'. There are a number of possible explanations available to us and the following examples have been taken directly from the dictionary:

> *'Halt or impede the progress or movement'*
> *'Make unsuitable for passage or progress by obstruction'*
> *'Interruption of normal physiological function'*
> *'Interrupt or cease a train of thought by competing thoughts or psychological suppression'*

Let's look at the definitions in slightly more detail.

'Halt or impede the progress or movement'. This is the definition I expected to find and I think this is basically the one which most Karate schools have in mind when it comes to blocking. Basically, it is about putting something in the way of somebody's punch, thereby halting or at least slowing it down sufficiently to take the power out of it and enable you to deal with it. Fair enough. Somewhat basic, and it requires a reaction to be faster than an action, but fair enough in early training.

'*Make unsuitable for passage or progress by obstruction*'. On first reading, this sounds very similar to the first explanation. However, on closer inspection this is much more about making something 'unsuitable' to strike than it is about putting something in the way. Now, I think we might be getting there. This requires a far higher level of skill than the rather 'agricultural' strategy of simply 'getting in the way'.

This is a form of 'blocking' that we see boxers and MMA fighters using all the time. The tight guard and subtle movement, ducks, weaves and bobs of the professional boxer make the head an 'unsuitable' target for their opponent. The tucked-in cover-up of the MMA fighter stuck on his back with his opponent either mounted or in his guard, is an attempt to make the head an 'unsuitable' target. And it works, which is why the old high—low combinations of stand-up fighting, designed to make an opponent drop his hands to enable a head shot, are equally applicable on the ground.

'*Interruption of normal physiological function*'. Now we're talking. Now we are the aggressors and yet we are still 'blocking' by interrupting our opponent's normal physiological functions. So how do we do that? Well, a kick in the head ought to do it. As would a thigh kick, or a hook to the body, a trip, a sweep, an elbow, a headbutt, etc, etc.

Already, by our own definition, blocking has become much more of an all-encompassing approach to fighting than simply putting an arm out to intercept a punch or a kick.

'*Interrupt or cease a train of thought by competing thoughts or psychological suppression*'. Now, I *really* like this one. Think back to any fights in any format you have ever watched and try and pinpoint an act of 'psychological suppression'.

If you are having any trouble at all watch UFC fighter Chuck Liddell psych people out in the Octagon before his fights. Watch any of the early Mike Tyson fights and see how he had people beaten long before a punch was even thrown. But my favourite of all time has to be the legendary 'Rumble in the Jungle' where, against all the odds, Muhammad Ali utterly destroyed the much larger and heavier George Foreman.

The Rumble in the Jungle took place in 1974 on 30 October, in what is now known as the Democratic Republic of the Congo (previously Zaire).

At that time Muhammad Ali was on something of a 'comeback' trail and it was already going badly. Suspended from boxing for three years following his refusal to join the United States army and fight in Vietnam, he was noticeably slower and many felt he wasn't the fighter he had once been. This opinion appeared to be well founded when he lost in turn to both Joe Frazier and Ken Norton.

Foreman, on the other hand, appeared unstoppable. He had beaten opponent after opponent and had totally destroyed both Frazier and Norton — the guys who had only recently beaten Ali. Foreman knocked Frazier down no less than seven times in the first two rounds and in the run-up to the Foreman–Ali fight, many people genuinely feared for Ali's safety.

Both men spent the summer of 1974 training in Zaire getting ready for the fight. Ali, however, also spent his time there winning the hearts and minds of the local people. He went on runs with the locals, appeared in villages around the country, did photo shoots with the kids and became a total hero in the process. Ali continually insulted and mocked Foreman during the run-up to the fight (commonplace nowadays but unique at that time) and during the fight Foreman was totally confused by the crowd's positive reaction to Ali, and negative reaction to him.

This and the crowd's now legendary call of 'Ali bumaye' (Ali kill him) shook Foreman's confidence and he was unable to defeat Ali on the night. Ali's performance in the ring was awesome, but many people agree that it was his performance outside it that ultimately won him the fight.

Psychological suppression at its finest.

In summary, blocking is a far more subtle and sophisticated endeavour than the simple one–two of traditional one-step ippon kumite. Blocking in its true sense incorporates ducks, weaves, redirection, unbalancing, strikes, blows and psychological intimidation.

And all of these devices and strategies are present within our kata. The basic intercept blocks and high impact of the early kata are readily apparent. So are the more subtle tai sabaki body evasion techniques of the later ones. Finally, psychological intimidation is evident in many of the kata where the practitioner simply moves into an aggressor's 'space' even before a technique is performed. If you watch some of the best competition kata performers in any style you will see intimidation permeating their performance through the deliberate outward manifestation of an indomitable spirit and dominating presence.

CHAPTER 6
STANCES

STANCES
CHAPTER 6

Stances — we all have them, we all use them and we all spend hours training in them. But are we training in them the correct way? Are we focusing on the right aspects? And what are they really for?

The martial arts in general, and Karate in particular, spend an awful lot of time working on stances and training in getting stances correct. But correct against what criteria? And to what end?

How is it that other combat-based disciplines, such as boxing, Judo or wrestling, spend little or no time looking at their stances and yet seem to function perfectly well? These disciplines definitely use stances but they don't appear to 'train' in them as such.

It is once again my contention that we in the Karate fraternity have lost our way somewhat with regard to the study and use of stances. We have become so focused on the micro issues of angles, distances and alignments that we have all but forgotten the macro issues of what the stances are for — effective transference of power along given lines of force.

The dictionary defines the word 'stance' to be '...a way of standing'. Yet we are training in a dynamic fighting system — why would we need so many 'ways of standing'?

Well, in order to address the question we might begin by looking at other, unrelated, disciplines that place heavy emphasis on the use of stances. Two that come to mind are dancing and golf. Classical dance teaches people to stand in exact ways — but for what function? Largely to make the dance beautiful — or to synchronise a lot of dancers into one overall aesthetically pleasing picture. To put it another way, they do it to make the piece look good. Could it be the case that this is what many of us have become?

What about golf then? Golfers spend a lot of time working on their stances. True enough, but then, they only have one function. The essence in the discipline of golf is to have one unswerving, unchanging, constant swing of the club. To deliver the club face to the ball in exactly the same manner, time after time after time.

One of the things that makes golf so fascinating / interesting / frustrating, is the fact that the target is completely stationary. Unlike the vast majority of other ball sports, the ball in golf is not moving. So the purpose of the stance is to deliver an unmoving angle of impact, to an unmoving target — very far removed from the world of combat. To deliver a powerful blow onto a moving, angry and hostile target is a world away from hitting a static target.

Of course we need some sort of ready stance — maybe even more than one since your ready stance when facing a boxer would have to be modified into a lower crouch when up against a grappler. But this already happens — naturally. Just look at the ready stances of boxers and grapplers and you will see that boxers have identifiably 'boxer's stances' and wrestlers have identifiably 'wrestler's stances'. And yet they spend very little time working on these stances. So how come they look so similar?

The answer lies in functionality. They stand the way they do because that is what works for them. Years of study have taught them the best way to stand to launch an attack on, or receive an attack from, the type of opponents they are trained to face. That being the case, of course they look similar.

Boxers are an interesting case in their own right. They may not spend much time working on *stances*, but they spent a lot of time working on *footwork*. This is where I believe we have wandered off the track a little. The stances that a boxer uses are part and parcel of the way that their bodies move in order to generate *powerful movement* and, more importantly, *powerful impact*. The power of the impact is a direct function of the correct stance but the *focus* of their training is the impact, not the stance.

So what are the benefits of training in static stances? Some people say that it teaches control. But control of what, and in what way? They say that it gives you strength in your legs. True, but standing in a static stance will only give you strength in that stance. The way to develop leg strength, as anyone familiar with weights will tell you, is to move through the whole movement range of the muscle (squats for example) – again, very far removed from a static approach. And they say that it teaches the correct posture. Also true. But it is teaching you a correct posture within an overall movement and so, at some stage the total movement must be taught and practised.

A lot of the way stances are taught in Karate dojos today has come from the Shotokan model. This is unsurprising as Shotokan is arguably the most popular style of Karate practised today. However, Shotokan is unique in that, according to its founder Gichin Funakoshi, its primary stated goal is the development of the spirit. Funakoshi held the development of the *spirit* over and above the development of the *fighter* or of fighting skills *per se*.

Consequently, Shotokan has a necessarily 'military' approach to training, and stances in this context are often used to put students into something approaching stress positions. Students are required to adopt very low stances and hold those stances for long periods of time. As a training method, this does an excellent job in developing spirit. But the functionality of the stance as a fighting platform has been superseded by the use of the stance to develop spirit within the practitioner.

It is a credit to Shotokan that so many Karate styles now emulate their training practices, but many do so without the knowledge of the overall goals, philosophy and ethos of Gichin Funakoshi and the inherent discipline of Shotokan.

The other problem is, of course, the way kata is trained and performed in large groups today. It is far easier to adjust the stance that somebody starts from or ends up in than it is to address the muscular-skeletal structures that drive the movement between these two stances. And yet it is here, in this movement, that the true value of the stance lies.

In this context 'Karate' stances are not unnatural, difficult or even unique. They are perfectly normal and everyday uses of body mechanics – again, just what the masters have been telling us all along.

Look at a fencer or a tennis player and you will see extensive use of zenkutsu dachi (the forward lunge stance). The tennis player will stretch to reach that open forehand while the fencer will lunge forward along a linear plane to target his opponent. Why do they do this? Because moving fast into zenkutsu dachi is the most efficient method for transferring power along the linear horizontal plane. These guys use the stance every bit as much as we do, they just don't have a name for it.

Look at a wrestler, grappler or Judo practitioner performing any number of grappling take-downs and you will recognise the low squatting stance of shiko or kiba dachi immediately. Why? Because practical use of shiko dachi is to either pick someone up or drag someone down, and the movement to or from shiko dachi is the most efficient way to transfer power along that vertical plane. They use the stance every bit as much as we do, they just don't have a name for it either.

Finally, look at a boxer working on a heavy bag and you will inevitably see him standing in the loose hour-glass stance of sanchin dachi. He does so because this is the most efficient way to stand if you want to deliver rotational power. All close-range hooks and uppercuts will come from this stance, as the alignment of hips, knees and feet dictate that this is the most efficient way to stand. Again, they just don't have a name for it.

So, am I saying that static stances should not be practised? No, not at all. The gift that the masters have given us is a minute breakdown of all the facets that go to make up the fighter. Our job is to piece it all together to produce strength, fluidity, power, efficiency and spirit. Static stances are indeed the start and end points of a given movement and, as such, they should be practised extensively. However, in order to transfer these learnings into applicable, street-practical fighting skills, equal or greater consideration must be given to the power lines associated with each stance, and to the all-important *movement between stances* — to the dynamic drive from one stance to another.

Goju Ryu kata are divided in two main groups: *Kaishugata* and *Heishugata*. The *Kaishugata* comprise Gekisai-Dai-Ichi, Gekisai-Dai-Ni, Saifa, Seiunchin, Shisochin, Sanseru, Sepai, Sesan, Kururunfa and Suparinpei. The *Heishugata* comprise Sanchin and Tensho.

CHAPTER 7 THE ROLE OF SANCHIN

Kaishugata and *Heishugata* literally translate as 'open-hand kata' and 'closed-hand kata' respectively, although, as both sets of kata use both open and closed hands, this is somewhat confusing. Ultimately, the actual hand position is just an analogy and whether your hands are open or closed is irrelevant – it is where you direct your attention that is important.

The real difference between the 'open' and the 'closed' kata is one of focus. Imagine that all of your attention, focus and energy is flowing through your body, down your arms, into your hands and into your fingertips. If your hands are open, all of that intent will be directed outwards. In the *Kaishugata* this is symbolic of attention to physical detail, aesthetic performance of the kata, and, of course, individual techniques. The *Kaishugata* are therefore 'external' kata.

If your hands are closed, all of that intent will be returned and directed inwards towards yourself. In the *Heishugata* (Sanchin and Tensho) this translates into looking inwards and a focus on the *principles* that underpin the techniques that we use. The 'closed' analogy is also symbolic of a focus on the internal aspects of our art. Sanchin is therefore an 'internal' kata.

Despite this, it would nevertheless be a mistake to view Sanchin as a purely spiritual endeavour. Sanchin has core fighting relevance. In fact, to pick up on Iain Abernethy's oak tree analogy in the foreword of this book, Sanchin is the acorn of Karate. Sanchin is the distillation and codification of all the principles and strategies you need to know – rooting, floating, sinking, spitting, swallowing, pushing, pulling, blocking, striking, throwing, lifting, unweighting, unbalancing, redirecting etc. are all contained within this incredible kata.

The four kata outlined in this book are all *Kaishugata* but this should in no way be taken to mean that Sanchin is not important. Sanchin is the distillation of the learnings of these kata and as such, it is easier to understand the message itself than it is the distillation of the message.

In order to truly understand what you are doing with Sanchin, you must have a clear understanding of the purposes, aims and goals of the training up to (and beyond) black belt. As such, it is both likely and desirable that you will be studying Sanchin in parallel to the training outlined in this book. Sanchin will be key to your ongoing understanding and development. However, the study of the *Heishugata* deserve (and require) a separate book in their own right and, at this stage, all the elements you require to build the complete fighter are contained within the initial four kata of the Goju syllabus and, indeed, within the following pages of this book.

PART 3 TH

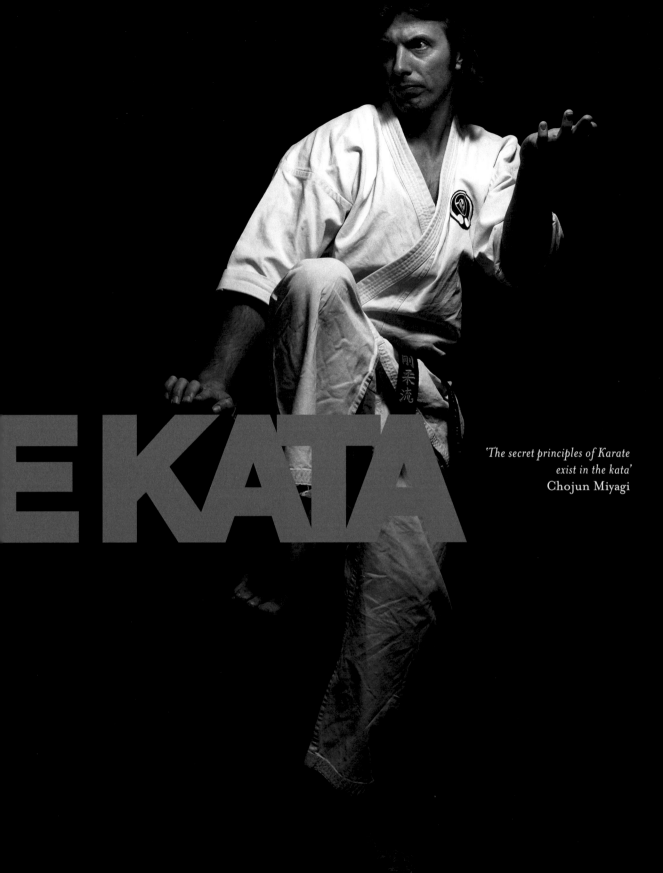

E KATA

'The secret principles of Karate
exist in the kata'
Chojun Miyagi

CHAPTER 8
ATTACK & SMASH
(GEKISAI-DAI-ICHI)

The Principle: *Straightforward blitzing attack*
The Mindset: *To overpower and overwhelm*
The Area of Combat: *Long to mid range, striking*

It's late and I'm walking home. I really should have got the last bus but she was cute and one more drink was just too tempting. Cold and hungry, it doesn't feel like such a good idea now. I walk past the graffiti-covered garages, past the homeless guy who asks me for change then curses me for saying nothing. I walk on, feeling a mixture of mild guilt and mild anger. I carry on, hands in my pockets, head down. That was a mistake and I see him too late. He's right in my face, spitting with fury. But I haven't done anything. It must be a mistake. He must think I'm someone else. My legs feel weak, I feel sick, and I can't think straight. Thank God he's more drunk than I am and I see him draw his right hand back. As he starts to swing at me I cover up and move in towards him. I lash out, almost blindly and, as much by luck as judgement, I catch him in the face and he goes down. I continue the momentum by stepping over him and I run as fast as I can until I get home. My heart is still beating fast, and not just from the running. I still feel sick and my hands won't stop shaking...

THE FIRST STEPS

Imagine this situation: A young lad walks nervously into your dojo and when you go over to speak to him you can see the faint yellow trace of a two-week-old black eye and the fading marks of various cuts and bruises on his face.

The kid has clearly been beaten up and despite what he tells you are his reasons for being there, the truth is he is seeking your help as a martial artist. More than that, he is seeking the assistance of the martial arts in general. He may know nothing about the martial arts, yet here he is. He is looking to you to ensure that the painful, terrifying and humiliating event that he was recently subjected to never happens to him again. Now that is a big responsibility you've just been landed with. What do you do?

Bear in mind that apart from his recent beating, he has probably had no experience of violence or violent confrontation in all of his 18 years on this planet. What is the first thing that you need to teach him? Fair enough, it's awareness, but what's next? In terms of physical strategy where do you start? Wrist locks? Arm bars? High kicks? Take-downs? Grappling skills? I don't think so.

The first thing you need to work on is developing an attacking, aggressive mindset and an indomitable spirit. You need to teach this lad to become an aggressive fighter using the simple, basic and often best tools of Karate: punches, kicks and strikes.

Basically, you need to teach him to attack and smash. You need to teach him Gekisai-Dai-Ichi.

PRINCIPLES OF GEKISAI-DAI-ICHI

The kanji (Japanese characters) for Gekisai-Dai-Ichi literally translate as *'Attack and Smash Number One'*. The 'essence' of this kata and the first area of study is indicated by the title itself. This is a 'Go' kata – a 'hard' kata. It is the start point in building the martial artist and it tells us what we need to do for the next six months or so. We need to study and investigate all manner of hard-style attack-and-smash techniques.

The range of Gekisai-Dai-Ichi is somewhat long. Some people have described this distance as 'striking distance' but I dislike that term as you can, and should, strike from any range. Other people (including myself) have talked about this range as somewhat unrealistic; however, what it really indicates is that we are right at the beginning of the fight progression. We have tried to avoid the conflict: we have done the stand-off where we have reiterated our unwillingness to go down this route; we have observed the ritual discourtesies; and now it has kicked off with a single big attack. We have not yet closed to grappling range, which might or might not happen depending on the skill and strategies of the two fighters involved, but right now we are looking at a snapshot in time, and the range is long.

Often when people talk about 'fighting' and 'self-defence', they separate them into two distinct camps, both of which are thought of differently and trained for differently. There is a good reason for this: a fight is generally thought of as a two-way exchange over a prolonged period of time, whereas self-defence is often viewed as a much faster, more brutal altercation. However, while this has got some truth to it, it is a mistake to separate the two quite so totally.

For example, it may be our intention to end the conflict in a fast two-second burst (self-defence). Nevertheless, best laid plans o' mice and men and you can easily find yourself struggling with one or more assailants for much longer than you hoped (a fight). Equally, even if the two protagonists are evenly matched, it may start off as a fight but degenerate into something much more one-sided and brutal as one gets the upper hand and starts to dominate the other.

There is a prevailing misunderstanding within some traditional martial arts schools that kumite somehow replicates a real fight. In truth it is arguably one of the least useful elements of traditional training when it comes to preparing for real contact. Fights simply do not involve two parties dancing around each other trying to get a shot in. Kumite does, of course, have its benefits (timing, movement, controlled chaos etc) and I am by no means suggesting that you should not do it; however, in truth, the majority of fights are over very quickly — much more like kata bunkai than dojo sparring. Another simple truth is that the victor is usually the one who manages to get in the first good solid shot. Horribly simple but, equally horribly, true.

Again, this is why your 'streetfighter', who in my experience is usually crap at fighting, is an extremely dangerous opponent. Having one or two strong opening techniques (headbutt, haymaker…) combined with sneakiness and distraction tactics (*'Got the time, mate?'*) is a totally devastating combination. No matter who you are, if you are suckered into glancing at your watch and as you look up you take a perfectly timed headbutt into your unexpecting and unclenched jaw, you are going down. It really is as simple as that. And what is the overall tactic of this untrained streetfighter? Clearly, and beyond any dispute, it is to attack and smash.

THE KATA: *Gekisai-Dai-Ichi*

Gekisai-Dai-Ichi begins from the 'ready stance' (centre-page) with a 90-degree turn to the left in left sanchin dachi and a left-hand jodan age uke, followed by stepping into right zenkutsu dachi and executing right jodan tsuki. Next, step back with the right foot 90 degrees into shiko dachi with a gedan barai over the left knee.

The entire sequence is then repeated to the right in opposite stances (i.e. right instead of left) ending up facing back in the starting direction.

Stepping into left sanchin dachi, perform left chudan uke with ibuki breathing tension. Step forward and repeat with right stance and block.

Execute a left chudan mae geri dropping into left zenkutsu dachi, followed by three techniques with the left hand: mae empi uchi, jodan uraken uchi and gedan barai, followed by right chudan gyaku tsuki.

Turn 90 degrees to the right and execute a right ashi barai landing in heiko dachi and delivering a right jodan yoko shuto uchi.
The chambered hand is closed. Following the direction of your striking hand, step forward into left sanchin dachi, perform a left
chudan uke, and then repeat the chudan mae geri into zenkutsu, empi uchi, jodan uraken uchi, gedan barai, chudan gyaku tsuki
combination using the right side instead of the left.

Repeat the ashi barai, heiko dachi, jodan yoko shuto uchi moves. Finally, step back into right zenkutsu dachi and deliver a double punch (awase tsuki), then change feet and perform a second awase tsuki. The lower hand is the one next to the leading leg. Yame to finish.

THE KIHON

Sadly, it seems some schools have failed to understand the links between all of the various elements of their training, and as a result kata, kihon, kumite, ne-waza (forms, basics, sparring, grappling) have largely come to be viewed as totally separate entities. In truth, these are the various strands that, while strong on their own, weave together to form a single entity whose strength is far greater than the sum of its individual parts. In other words, all elements should be working together in a progressive manner to help mould, shape and guide the student towards becoming a well-rounded martial artist and a competent fighter.

Therefore, it is crucial that any kihon training undertaken is in complete harmony with the spirit of the kata being studied at that time. And the reason for this is mindset.

The emergence of the limited rules of MMA in the early 1990s shook the martial arts world and events like the UFC forced people to examine what they were doing with a number of different outcomes.

On the positive side, some people liked the competition format and switched over to MMA combat-sport style training. Others saw and respected it for what it was — an incredibly tough and skilful ring sport for those athletes who wished to fight like-minded people in a limited rules format.

However, there were also some more negative reactions. Some chose to withdraw into themselves, shutting themselves off totally from the rest of the martial arts community and refusing to see what was happening before their eyes. Others simply panicked and started flailing around trying to strap on some groundwork / grappling / striking / high kicks / low kicks, whatever, to try to plug what they now perceived as gaps in their own styles. And the main problem with this approach is mindset.

For example, imagine you had a hard-core Karate system which focused heavily on effective striking but, for one reason or another, had omitted evasion and throwing for the last fifty years or so. Little Billy notices this gap and so sets off to do some Aikido to tack on to his Karate. The problem is not in the techniques that he will learn — there are some awesome Aikido techniques and, delivered by a master, I have no doubt as to their potential. The problem lies in the mindset which underpins those techniques — one being to meet force with more force and punch someone unconscious, the other being to blend with that force and become a part of it — to harmonise with it.

Of course in the higher levels, you need to develop both of these attributes and be able to switch between them. However, remember we are at a very early stage in the development of our potential martial artist and confusing messages over mindset and ethos are not going to help.

Therefore, while the new student is in the attack-and-smash phase of his training, all elements of his training must follow this theme in order to develop the indomitable spirit which we are setting out to forge.

Kihon at this stage should therefore focus on hard straight attacks, primarily emphasising the punches, kicks, sweeps and elbows outlined in Gekisai-Dai-Ichi. What is definitely *not* required at this stage is the higher level concepts of evasion, trapping, manipulation and redirection. We are firing this boy straight down the middle — the straight blast, to borrow a Wing Chun term.

It may not be sophisticated. It may not be pretty. But it is effective and it is effective in a relatively short period of time which is why it is most definitely the place to start.

THE BUNKAI

The story is exactly the same for the bunkai. Most schools will have a basic set of bunkai for each kata and that's fine. The main problem with the bunkai is that the exceptional work of people like Iain Abernethy in reviving the original, realistically combat-effective bunkai from the Wado system has been misinterpreted in some sectors to mean that any given move can mean *anything* at all. This is, of course, nonsense — not as bad as some of the kata interpretation we've all seen, but nonsense nonetheless.

To have any value in helping to progress the martial artist, the bunkai contained within a given kata must reflect the 'spirit' of that particular kata. As such, the bunkai we are seeking from Gekisai-Dai-Ichi must reflect the mindset of attack-and-smash. We are looking for hard-line, linear techniques of mass destruction.

PADWORK DRILLS

At this stage, padwork drills should focus on power, impact and tenacity. Yes, tenacity. Remember what it is that we are trying to develop at this stage of training, and a big part of that is developing the 'never-give-up muscle'.

In a recent interview by Jamie Clubb for his book on the 'reality revolution' of the 1990s, his very first challenge was this:

'Put the following in order of importance: Awareness, Accuracy, Knockout power, Conviction, Attitude, Technique, Principles, General conditioning.'

I bet a pound to a penny that anyone who knows the first thing about confrontation will have the first two down as being 'Awareness' and 'Attitude'. So, leaving awareness aside, the first thing you need to teach someone is attitude, and a lot of that attitude can be developed through correct and gruelling use of the pads.

Apart from teaching how to hit, and how to hit hard, we are attempting to develop this indomitable spirit that we spoke about earlier.

At this stage, therefore, padwork should be technical only in respect of getting the correct alignment of body and wrist for power and to prevent injury. The rest is all about punching to destruction. In this case, self-destruction. So one minute full-on, non-stop. Thirty second rest. Two minutes full-on. One minute rest. Three minutes full-on. One and a half minutes rest... and so on.

As an additional benefit you will also find that the students develop a much more natural punching style. Exhaustion is a very useful tool. One of the things you notice when somebody untrained first starts to hit the pads is how stiff and tense they are. This stiffness needs to be eliminated before the student can start to develop real power on impact. You can tell some people a thousand times to loosen up and relax and they will still never get it. However, if they have been punching non-stop for three minutes, they will simply be too tired to maintain a stiff and tense body and so you can go to work. Job done in three minutes.

PARTNER DRILLS

Useful as all the individual work and supplementary exercises undoubtedly are, there is no substitute for working with a live opponent/partner.

In order to progress quickly, safely and with some mates into the bargain, one of the very first things you need to identify, and identify correctly, is when the person standing in front of you is an opponent and when he is a partner. Given that this is often the same person, this may sound like a facile remark, but I couldn't be more serious.

One of the single biggest barriers to progression in the martial arts is trying to 'beat' everybody else in the dojo. By trying to 'win' all the time you fall into the trap of only using your best (hence most familiar and 'winning') techniques. This restricts you from developing your weaker attributes. Furthermore, fewer and fewer people will be willing to train with you. This severely limits the range of your martial experience. And finally, those who *can* beat you invariably will. They will pick up on your vibe and put you in your place time and time again. Don't get me wrong, there are some major learnings to be taken away from such a scenario but it will seriously limit the extent of actual 'teaching' you receive from the higher grades.

So it's a fine distinction but one to get on top of right from the outset.

With your training partner firmly in 'partner' mode, develop some kumite drills which emphasise direct-line attack. The three-step sparring drill (shown below) is ideal:

> *Square off as in sparring*
> *Attack with a solid contact left punch—right punch combination to the body followed by a low round kick to the lead thigh*
> *The receiver 'absorbs' the blows but does not try to block or evade*
> *Then it's their go*
> *Carry on turn for turn, gradually increasing power and movement*

The benefits of these types of drill are that the student immediately begins to ingrain a very useful fight pattern into their mind and muscles. If the shit hits the fan, you could do much worse than drive forward with a left—right—low kick combination.

Obviously, as the drill progresses, pick up the movement, pace, power and, most importantly, the intent within the exercise.

You can, of course, add inside thigh kicks, knees and elbows but it really isn't about techniques at this stage. It's just about developing that very simple mindset of attacking and smashing an opponent with one or two very simple tools.

CONDITIONING

Supplementary training (hojo undo) has always been an integral part of the traditional ways of building a martial artist and at this stage of the student's development, we need to look at the hojo undo equipment available, keeping in mind what we are trying to achieve. We are talking about using solid attacks with fists and feet and there is one crucial piece of equipment that is specifically designed to equip us to do that job – the makiwara.

Simply put, the makiwara is a striking post. This is an invaluable piece of equipment but one which has come under much criticism in recent times. While it is true that incorrect use of the makiwara will result in physical damage, so would incorrect use of a bench press, heavy bag, or a Bo for that matter. In fact, I would go so far as to say that punching thin air has damaged far more Karate students than hitting the makiwara ever has. Rather than throw the baby out with the bath water, the key is to find out how to use this equipment correctly.

It is a common misconception that the goal of makiwara training is to produce calloused knuckles which are impervious to impact. It is true that this can happen, but there is far more to the makiwara than simply conditioning the hands.

By now, I would hope that everybody is familiar with the damage that can be done to ligaments and joints by repeatedly 'snapping' techniques into the open air. Moreover, punching air simply develops, encourages and exacerbates bad habits as there is nothing in the exercise against which success might be measured. As we have seen, simply punching thin air can only ever teach you the 'trigger' part of a punch. It can never give you any feedback on power, penetration or impact, and it can never give you the true feeling of actually striking an opponent. Combine that with 'semi-contact' sparring and we are in a real mess. We are training, grading and promoting karateka who have never hit, and who have no hope of ever developing the ability to hit, anything.

Padwork and heavy bag training are fantastic for developing correct striking attributes and many would argue that their benefits outweigh those of the makiwara. However, while I am a big advocate of pads and the heavy bag, I still believe that the makiwara offers something fundamentally different.

It is an unfortunate truth that many fights consist almost exclusively of people tying to punch each other in the head. As the thickest bone in the body, the skull is not the ideal target for an unconditioned hand. Boxers often break their hands if they are forced to strike bare knuckle as they are simply not conditioned to strike in this manner – a closed fist in a boxing glove is actually a relatively loose and 'open' fist. As karateka we are primarily bare-knuckle fighters and our hands need to be conditioned in order to take on that job.

While the head may be a risky target, it is without any doubt, your best chance of ending the fight with a knockout. Therefore it is imperative that your hands are conditioned to resist the force of the impact you have developed over time, otherwise the first time you punch someone in the head may be the last time you use that hand during that fight – not a good start.

The makiwara addresses this problem by working on your stance, alignment and coordination; by strengthening the arms, wrists and hands; and by ultimately conditioning the small bones and knuckles of the striking hand.

There are other pieces of traditional equipment that serve similar purposes to the makiwara in that they seek to condition the striking surfaces of the body, for example the 'tou' (stick bundle) and the 'jari bako' (sand bowl) but for now, the makiwara is king.

THE NEXT STAGE

Hopefully, by now our new student will have put his original beating behind him. He is now capable of hard solid attacks and his mind is growing stronger. The low-lifes who made him feel so worthless no longer keep him awake at night and he no longer trains with revenge in his heart. Now he trains because he loves it.

When he first arrived he would simply give up when he could do no more sit-ups or push-ups, now he'll dig deep to get that last one out. His spirit is developing well but we need to increase the realism of the fight. And we do that by moving the fight closer.

The range will still be relatively long but he's no longer going to get away with such a simplistic and direct attack; before smashing his opponent he's now going to need to get out of the way.

He's ready for Gekisai-Dai-Ni — Attack and Smash Number Two.

CHAPTER 9
ATTACK & SMASH 2
(GEKISAI-DAI-NI)

The Principle: *Pull/push, unbalancing and redirection*
The Mindset: *To evade and overpower*
The Area of Combat: *Closer range, striking*

I hate stag nights. I've always hated stag nights but sometimes you have to do your duty to your mates. I also hate clubs but here I am, tired, hot and almost deaf. To make matters worse, I'm driving and supposed to look after this drunken idiot next to me. Man, I just should have said no when he first asked me. I was enjoying myself until about twenty minutes ago when my mate tripped over his own feet and knocked into these three guys. There was a lot of chest puffing but I bought them a beer and it all seemed to calm down. £12.60 for three beers — I hate clubs. Any sense of fun is long gone and I just want to go home. I have been half-watching them ever since and I can see them heading over. The hairs on the back of my neck stand up and this looks bad. I look around for the bouncers. Damn it! They're there quick enough if you've got a pair of trainers on but now when you need them... One of the guys pushes my mate who staggers and just looks confused. People move away and a space clears around us so I step into it and try to talk to the bloke — maybe appeal to his better nature. I look into his eyes and can see that his better nature took a rain check about five beers ago. There is only one way this is going down. He reaches for me with his left hand. I am painfully aware of the bottle in his right so I slap his reaching hand across his body, check his elbow with my left and throw a big right hander to the side of his jaw. He goes down like a sack of shit and his bottle smashes on the floor. The bouncers are on me in a flash (bastards must have been watching all along) and I quickly find myself out on the street, closely followed by my mate. I want to get my coat but the bouncers are having none of it so we just head off to find a taxi. Shit, I've never knocked anyone out before. Man that feels good...

PRINCIPLES OF GEKISAI-DAI-NI

The kanji for Gekisai-Dai-Ni literally translate as *'Attack and Smash Number Two'*. The 'essence' of this kata and the second area of study is again indicated by the title itself. This is still a hard kata. We are still studying and investigating all manner of hard-style attack-and-smash techniques. However, this time we see the introduction of open-handed and evasive techniques and strategies.

It's time to learn how to get out of the way.

The second Gekisai kata appears to have proved something of a problem for some Goju schools around the world. It seems that some people have had trouble figuring out exactly what it is that they are supposed to be doing with it. The problem is that apart from two basic moves, Gekisai-Dai-Ichi and Gekisai-Dai-Ni are practically identical.

This has led to a number of different conclusions and strategies being reached over the years:

1. Some decided that Gekisai-Dai-Ni was really the same as Gekisai-Dai-Ichi but kept on teaching it anyway just to keep everything 'traditional'. However, in practice they really just skip over it quickly to get to the next 'real' kata.

2. Others perceived the second kata to be adding only very small incremental learnings and so added on a few more versions; Gekisai-Dai-San (3) Gekisai-Dai-Yon (4) and Gekisai-Dai-Go (5) all exist.

3. Still others concluded that the second kata wasn't really teaching anything new and so dropped it from their syllabus.

However, the truth is that despite only having two moves different from the first kata, the second one is *entirely different*. And the reason that some have missed this fact is that the difference is not to be found in the actual *movements* of the kata – the difference lies in the range of combat.

This kata is a step closer to the action and the presence of open-handed techniques and 45-degree evasive movement confirms that this is the case.

Remember that moving onto your next kata doesn't simply mean you have another dance to learn. It is telling you the specific area of combat which you need to study for the next year or so. So what are we looking at?

We are going to spend the next phase of our training learning to evade attacks and to gain a tactical advantage over our opponent through movement and positioning. Furthermore, we are going to be acquiring that positional advantage through 'receiving' a technique instead of blocking it (the actual meaning of '*uke*') and by so doing, we are going to learn how to manipulate our opponent into a position of weakness.

THE KATA: *Gekisai-Dai-Ni*

Just like Gekisai-Dai-Ichi, the second kata begins from a ready stance (centre page) with a 90-degree turn to the left in left sanchin dachi and a left-hand jodan age uke, followed by stepping into right zenkutsu dachi and executing a right jodan tsuki. Next, step backwards with the right foot 90 degrees into shiko dachi with a gedan barai over the left knee. The entire sequence is then repeated to the right in opposite stances ending up facing back in the starting direction.

Stepping into left sanchin dachi, perform left chudan uke (this part and the following sequence is not shown). Step forward and repeat with right stance and block. Next is a left chudan mae geri stepping into left zenkutsu dachi, followed by three techniques with the left hand: mae empi uchi, jodan uraken uchi and gedan barai, followed by right chudan gyaku tsuki. As before, turn 90 degrees to the right and execute a right ashi barai landing in heiko dachi and delivering a right jodan yoko shuto uchi. This time the chambered hand is open.

Following the striking hand, step into left sanchin dachi, perform a left hiki uke. Step forward into right sanchin and perform a right kake uke, rapidly stepping back into left sanchin and performing a left hiki uke.

Repeat the chudan mae geri, empi uchi, jodan uraken uchi, gedan barai, chudan gyaku tsuki combination using the right side instead of the left.

Repeat the ashi barai, heiko dachi, jodan yoko shuto uchi moves. From heiko dachi, slide the left foot back on a 45-degree angle into right neko ashi dachi while performing mawashi uke and tora guchi.

Then use suri ashi to slide the right foot to the opposite side at 45 degrees from the centre and repeat with mawashi uke and tora guchi. Maintain your position and focus to the front. Yame to finish.

THE KIHON

Once again we must keep in mind that we are working to a system and are not simply bolting disparate elements of training together any which way. The student is still in the attack-and-smash phase of his training and all elements of his training must follow this theme. We have already come a long way since that frightened kid first came into our dojo, but we are far from done with developing the indomitable spirit that we have started to forge in our young protégé.

So, while the tactics and strategies emphasised at this point will change from pure linear attacks to evasive, reactive attacks, the *mindset* will not change and it must remain attack-and-smash in nature. Kihon at this stage should therefore focus on absorbing-receiving- and redirecting-type movements and blocks followed by hard smashing attacks. In addition to the punches, kicks, sweeps and elbows emphasised in Gekisai-Dai-Ichi, primary weapons now include open-handed shuto, taisho, haito strikes and blocks, as well as use of the forearms to intercept, smash and demolish an attacker.

Kihon drills should be similar to those used in Gekisai-Dai-Ichi but plenty of use must be made of angled 45-degree stances, fast-hip neko ashi-type evasion, as well as open-handed blocking and striking.

While the mindset at this stage may not change, the skill levels required to achieve the goals laid out in the kata are significantly higher. Concepts of evasion, positioning and redirection are high-level concepts and definitely not something to be dropped from the syllabus or skipped over in a half-hearted fashion. Believe me, to develop as a fighter, you need evasive ability. You need Gekisai-Dai-Ni.

THE BUNKAI

Naturally, the bunkai must now express elements of evasion before counter-attack.

Some are, of course, more obvious than others. For example, we have the three-step hiki-uke, kake-uke, hiki-uke combination in the middle. We also have the two neko-ashi mawashi-uke movements at the end. All open-handed and all easily interpretable as redirectional blocks and/or strikes.

However, while that is all well and good, we should still seek the 'spirit' of the kata in the other movements. For many years I failed to grasp this basic principle and had students just *'show me the differences between Gekisai-Dai-Ichi and Gekisai-Dai-Ni'*. That is to say, I had made the classic error of assuming that because the opening moves were the same, so were the bunkai. On reflection, while that may be understandable, it is clearly nonsense and lazy to boot.

Let's take the very first sequence of moves for both kata: both start with a 90-degree turn to the left with a left-hand upper block, followed by stepping into right zenkutsu dachi and punching right jodan gyaku tsuki.

In Gekisai-Dai-Ichi, the bunkai might be very literal, starting with the defender standing at 90 degrees to the attacker. As the attacker lunges in with a straight right, the defender turns and blocks with his left arm before powering forward and hitting him in the face with a powerful gyaku tsuki. Straightforward attack and smash.

For Gekisai-Dai-Ni, however, we need to make this a little more realistic. So, for example, we might start with the two guys facing off. The attacker comes in with a classic left—right combination. The defender parries the left punch inwards with the covering (right) hand while moving slightly to the right. As the right punch comes in the defender blocks the attacker's swinging right arm with his left arm.

In this instance the circular motion of the hands puts the attacker in a momentarily bad position and creates an opening right in front of him. As this gap will clearly not be there for very long, the defender must immediately go into offensive mode and once again power through that opening with total attack-and-smash aggression.

Notice that in the first instance, our attack was almost instinctive and was more or less a straightforward reactive drive into the attacker. In the second instance we set ourselves up with positioning and evasion before launching a devastating counter attack. Both could work well but the second has a greater chance of success owing to positional advantage gained early on in the encounter.

So while the kata moves may be identical, one is utilising a much higher level of skill to deliver the *coup de grâce* and that is the forte of Gekisai-Dai-Ni.

PADWORK DRILLS

At this stage we still need to be focusing on power and impact; however, we need to incorporate elements of ducking, slipping and generally evading before, after and during strikes.

As the student has presumably progressed over the last few months he should already be hitting harder. As such, correct alignment of the hand, wrist and forearm are essential if injury is to be avoided. There are four key areas where the correct fist can be developed.

Firstly, careful attention must have been paid to the structure of the fist during kihon. Basically, unlike boxing, the karateka is aiming to impact with the first two knuckles of the punching hand. Kihon in the early stages should emphasise the correct alignment of knuckles through forearm to shoulder. This is one of the primary uses of kihon. There is an awful lot wrong with punching in mid-air; however, you do have a snapshot in time with which to assess and fine-tune the alignment of the fist before making the student hit something heavy. Once a student has progressed to hitting solid objects, however, these minute adjustments during kihon are all but redundant.

Secondly, the solidity of the fist structure can be developed via correct use of knuckle push-ups. Again, we are working towards a system and all the pieces of the jigsaw must fit together. While we do use push-ups to develop strength and stamina, this is not their main purpose. Push-ups are used in Karate to develop the never-give-up muscle, to strengthen and align the wrist—fist combination, and to ingrain a dynamic stretch reflex that releases a fast, powerful punch. The first objective is easy — just do lots of them. The second and third require a little more attention to detail.

If you are seeking to ingrain some of the elements of a punch, then the push-up must follow the same path as your punch. Thus for example, a gyaku tsuki is far better mimicked and served if push-ups are done with the elbows close to the body — not, as you so often see, with the arms bent out like a crocodile. If you do this you only get the benefits of strength and developing the never-give-up muscle.

Furthermore, if we are seeking to replicate the stretch—reflex trigger of a punch, the push-up must mimic this. That is to say you should not lower yourself down and up in the steady fashion of a fitness guru. You need to be dropping your body weight in order to reverse it fast, and with as much power as possible, at the bottom of the push-up. This way your push-up becomes an extremely useful tool. Now, not only are you developing strength *per se*, you are also directly affecting your punching power — perfect.

The third area of development will be in the use of makiwara. Any flaws in angle or structure of the wrist will soon be revealed by this most eloquent of teachers.

Finally, heavy bag work will help to develop power and penetration in your punch while revealing any flaws in structure due to angled punches which would be missed by the solid flat face of the makiwara.

So, once we are sure that the student will be able to hit with power while not sustaining any injury to wrists, forearms or hands, we can progress with the drills.

Now, instead of simple one-two type progressions, the one holding the pad should pepper the drills with trying to strike the person punching. Jabs to slip, long looping haymakers to duck etc. Drills should also emphasise a lot of footwork, and have the student clear one pad in order to strike the other.

In this way we are moving the student beyond the simple linear attack into a more sophisticated positioning, redirection, set-up and movement based attacking style.

PUSHING HANDS (KAKIE)

It is at this stage of the student's training that one of the most fundamentally useful tools in self-defence or martial arts in general should be introduced – pushing hands.

Pushing hands (also known as 'kakie' in the Okinawan martial arts) involves two people (sometimes three) crossing arms at the wrists or forearms. Maintaining constant contact, a rhythmical pattern of pushing and redirecting is established between the two students with the aim of understanding and 'feeling' each other's energy. It is basically a sensitivity drill and fundamental to all reality-based martial arts.

In the sometimes over-macho world of the martial arts, words and concepts involving 'sensitivity' are often undervalued, if not rejected outright. This, however, is a big mistake. Pushing hands is without doubt one of the most practical and important self-defence drills that there is. Why? Because it's all about yielding, blending the hard with the soft, the Go with the Ju, Yin and Yang, swallowing and spitting, floating and sinking. It's all about accepting the force and evading it at the same time. It's all about redirecting the opponent and using their own force against them – classic martial strategy.

Pushing hands also contains another crucially important self-defence concept; muchimi – 'sticking' hands. The principle of sticking to an opponent and not breaking contact until you decide to do so is extremely sound.

The aim of pushing hands is to develop sensitivity to your partner's movements and intentions. By becoming sensitive to changes in his energy, you are then able to redirect his strength and force against him to your strategic advantage. The basic principle is one of harmony and some people talk about the concept of 'investing in loss'. In this case, yielding and giving space in order to acquire an overall advantage.

During practice you must really 'listen' to your partner's body movements. Pushing hands teaches the student to read subtle body signs and sensations. After a while the student should try to anticipate movements before they even happen, and once the movement is made, the force should be redirected and channelled through the body and then neutralised or returned to your partner. This is the essence of pushing-hands.

Clearly, we are already talking about some pretty high-level principles and our guy has only been here six months. The truth is that at Gekisai-Dai-Ni level, these concepts are really only hinted at. However, like much in the martial arts, many years of study will be required in order to master the concepts and the sooner the student starts off on the correct path the better.

There are probably as many variations of Okinawan kakie as there are of Chinese pushing hands. However, the most common form is a single-handed version very similar to the Chinese chi sau.

Standing in loose sanchin dachi, face your partner and cross your right arms at the wrists. The aim is to describe an arc vertically between you, from your sternum to theirs. There should be no jerky movements, no acceleration and no real resistance as such – simply a constant pressure allowing for the free exchange of energy and 'feel'. As you push forward, rotate your palm out. As you receive your partner's energy, rotate your palm towards your body. Absorb your partner's energy through your arm, down your body and into your back leg before reflecting the energy back up the same path and back into your partner.

The single biggest mistake newcomers to kakie make is to use excessive force, trying to push hard against an opponent – possibly even trying to 'beat' him. Avoid this at all costs.

Once the student has mastered the basic pattern
and principle of the drill you can add grabbing,
pulling, unbalancing, trips, sweeps etc. As ever, the
fighting techniques can be divided into categories;
for example, kansetsu waza (manipulation of the
joints), nage waza (throwing techniques), shime
waza (strangles and chokes) and kyusho waza
(manipulation of the vital points). Though, of
course, these elements are still to come at this stage
in the student's development. Kakie needs to focus
on movement intended to create an opening for a
blitzing attack.

A good way of ensuring that the practice of kakie is
done at the correct level of kata development is to take
the bunkai applications from Gekisai-Dai-Ichi and
Gekisai-Dai-Ni and apply them during kakie practice.

The sensitivity and close-range skills developed from
pushing hands training will be something the student
will value for the rest of his life. The old adage that
'practice makes perfect' is fundamentally flawed. What
practice does is perfect what you are practising. If that
is wrong in the first place you will *never* get it right.
Ensure that the student has a firm grasp of the basic
movement, principles and concepts of kakie before
moving them forward and you will have set them well
and truly on the path to becoming a martial artist in
their own right.

CONDITIONING

As with Gekisai-Dai-Ichi, we are still in a phase of hardening and toughening our basic impact weaponry. For this reason, the makiwara will still play a major part in our supplementary exercises (hojo undo).

Now, however, in addition to developing the knuckles (seiken) the student should progress to include the knife-edge of the hand (shuto).

As with any piece of equipment, there is a risk of injury if the exercises are not done correctly. Crucial here is the position of the open hand. The totally *incorrect* (and hence extremely dangerous) way to hold the striking hand is completely flat. Rather the hand should be cupped so that the bones in the hand can compress over one another, as opposed to banking together on impact. Finally the fingers should be arched away from the back of the hand and bent slightly to apply the correct tension to the striking edge.

Practice should start with the striking surface already in contact with the makiwara. Just by twisting the hips and generating power, the student should attempt to move the makiwara (it is crucial that the makiwara have a reasonable degree of 'give' in it. Too hard and it will result in injury). Once the student has a feel of the forces that are likely to be exerted on his hand, arm and body, striking can begin.

As ever, this is a long-term endeavour and training must be heavy and slow. Power and conditioning will come with time. Pain and injury will come with haste.

The second piece of traditional equipment that the student needs to be introduced to at this stage is the much hated and rightly feared chi'ishi: now here is a piece of equipment worth celebrating. After the makiwara, I value the chi'ishi above all other pieces of hojo undo equipment.

The chi'ishi consists of a heavy stone weight stuck on the end of a short wooden stick. Literally translated, chi'ishi means *'strength stone'*, although I have heard students refer to them as *'that big stone bastard on a stick'*. The chi'ishi is possibly the one piece of traditional resistance training equipment that has no direct equivalent to be found in a modern weights gym.

Offering a wide variety of exercises, the chi'ishi is basically used for strengthening the grip, wrists, shoulders and arms. However, its uses go way beyond those basics and used correctly, it can really be used to work whole muscle groups at once as the device is lifted, rotated, extended and retracted.

Its most basic pattern sees the practitioner in shiko dachi with the chi'ishi held straight down between the legs. One rep consists of the practitioner rotating the chi'ishi *towards the body* (a crucial element), and into the upright position at arm's length before returning along the same path to the vertical down start position. This pathway exercises and develops a set of muscles and tendons along a pathway totally ingrained in any martial artist's muscle memory as it is training the exact muscles used to block, throw, choke and strike. A fantastic piece of equipment.

However, at this stage we are using the chi'ishi with the specific aim of strengthening the body, and particularly the arms and wrists for what is about to come...

THE NEXT STAGE

So, what do we have now? Well, so far we have taken someone with no concept of how to fight and ingrained in him one basic strategy — attack and smash. He began by learning a straightforward response (direct and hard counter-attack) to a straightforward attack.

We then started to refine this strategy by including the elements of movement and evasion, redirection and positioning necessary to make this strategy a viable option in a real attack situation.

Alongside the basic fight strategy, we have begun to harden both the body and the mind through correct and progressive use of the grading system and of hojo undo (supplementary) training equipment and drills. So, guess what? It's time to turn up the heat... And we do that how? We do that by once again moving the fight closer.

Now we are getting into a much more realistic fighting range. We are moving into the range where he can be grabbed by an attacker. Attack-and-smash can be neutralised by such a strategy so he's going to need to know how to break free of a grab and get the fight back to the range he is now confident in.

He's ready for the next stage. He's ready for Saifa — tearing.

CHAPTER 10
TEARING
(SAIFA)

The Principle: *Escape from a grab by directing*
force against a weaker area
The Mindset: *Wrench free and attack*
The Area of Combat: *Grabs and holds*

I can hear the commotion getting louder at the back of the bus. I really don't want to get involved but what started off as piss-taking sounds like it's taken a nastier turn. There's a black lad on the bus with his white girlfriend and, like the rest of us, they just want to go home. These four guys got on about three stops ago and were being loud and obnoxious to everybody. However, they've now stopped abusing all and sundry and seem to have found their victim for the night. I'm really uncomfortable with this. Racist abuse really bothers me and the kid is only about 16 years old. I've got to say something. 'Just leave him alone,' I say half-heartedly. They laugh at me and I feel bad. Everybody else is pretending that nothing is happening so I do the same. I'd like to do more but there's four of them so what can I do anyway? I'm trying to justify my own inaction but deep down I'm not convinced and I feel like a coward. At the next stop the two kids get off. Do they thank me? No way. Just goes to show I was right not to get involved... only I am. One of the lads has moved down the bus. 'What did you say to me?' I look out of the window, attempting to look cool but my heart is racing and I'm sure everyone can hear it. 'I said, what did you say, shithead?' I remember reading once that bullies will just go away if you ignore them. I knew that was bullshit even then... Suddenly, his hands are on me and I'm yanked from my seat. He has both hands on my lapels and I can smell the alcohol on his breath. I reach over his left hand with my right. Hook it under his right hand, grab my own wrist and twist violently to my right. He is yanked forward and I'm free from his grasp. I pivot back and smash him full in the face with my elbow as the bus pulls up at the next stop. He staggers back into his mates who can't get past him. I jump off the bus and run as fast as I can. I have no idea where I am but I just keep running...

PRINCIPLES OF SAIFA

Saifa is made up of two kanji: *'sai'* and *'ha'* (the Okinawan pronunciation of ha is 'fa'). Sai means to 'smash' (as in Geki-*sai*), *fa* means to 'tear'. Saifa therefore means *'smash and tear'* and is of Chinese origin.

Up until now we have only dealt with striking attacks. In our first few months of study an attacker would lunge in with a punch or a kick and we would fight fire with fire by replying in much the same manner (Gekisai-Dai-Ichi).

As our skills improved, we moved the fight in a step closer to the point where a lunging attack would be slipped, parried or redirected before moving in for a decisive finish (Gekisai-Dai-Ni).

While we have closed the distance from long range to a closer, redirectional range, the next step in the fight progression is to move close enough to be grabbed. This is Saifa range and this kata, and hence the area of study for the next year or so, is all about fighting techniques and principles for breaking free of all manner of grabs and holds.

Stories are often told about how the founder of a style would not teach *all* of his students *all* of the kata. We often hear how certain individuals were only taught one or two kata. This has puzzled people for years as the assumption was made that some poor sod was left trying to perfect a single form for years and years. However, what was really being done was simply to play to people's strengths. So a good strong stand-up fighter might have stayed with the Gekisais, whereas a short stocky student might have been better off perfecting his grappling and staying in the Seiunchin phase of his training.

Each kata has its own character, and its concepts, strategies and tactics will each suit a different type of fighter.

For a good example of a Saifa fighter versus a Seiunchin fighter take a look at any of the epic UFC clashes between Randy Couture (Seiunchin) and Chuck Liddell (Saifa/Gekisai). While a good striker in his own right, Couture's real specialism was to grapple, ground and pound, and submit his opponents (Seiunchin — trapping battle). Liddell, on the other hand, although more than competent on the ground, specialised in frustrating grapplers by preventing their take-downs, tearing free of their grabs and holds (Saifa — tearing) and getting the fight back to the stand-up striking range he wanted (Gekisai — attack and smash).

It's not that one area is superior to another, it just depends who you are and what you want to do. However, to be a totally rounded fighter you need to study all areas and ranges of combat which is exactly what the progression of the kata does for you.

The vast majority of male-on-male attacks begin with a strike of some description — usually a right-hand punch or a headbutt. That is not the case for male-on-female attack (or indeed female-on-female attack). What happens in this situation is that, more often than not, the female is grabbed in some fashion — often by the arms or wrists by a male, often by the hair by a female. Saifa is therefore a crucial kata in what is often termed 'self-defence' because its primary goal is to escape.

The key to escaping from holds and grabs is positioning and leverage. Well, actually, it's just leverage because to get the necessary leverage to break the hold, you invariably need to get the position first. This will become increasingly important in the next stage of your training (Seiunchin) when you will often find yourself on the ground, either on top of or underneath an opponent.

However, for the time being, the fight is still standing. Although the principles still hold firm, Saifa is more concerned with that first early attack than it is about the cut, thrust and chaos that can ensue. This is because the principles of tearing which we will learn over the next year or so will still be totally relevant when we get to the full clinch-work of Seiunchin. At this stage, however, we are often starting from a simple grab and going from there.

One of the questions that haunts women involved in 'self-defence' as opposed to the martial arts, is how can a seven stone woman escape the clutches of a 14-stone man? Some even doubt that this can be done. I am never going to tell anyone that any element of fighting is easy — it isn't — but it can be done. In the days before weight divisions in the UFC, Royce Gracie was beating all comers in the Octagon when he was only about 12 stone.

The principle is to apply as much of that 7 stone as possible to the weakest part of the hold, and the way to make that work, is to use strikes and distractions as the force is applied.

Saifa has these in abundance.

THE KATA: *Saifa*

From the ready position (centre-page) Saifa begins by clasping the right fist in the left hand while taking a long step forward with the right foot, followed by bringing the left foot into musubi dachi and turning the body 90 degrees to the left.

Next, rip the hands from the right to the left side, still looking forward to the front, step back with the left foot into shiko dachi, and perform a left osae uke and a right jodan uraken uchi. Execute the same movements to the opposite (left) side, and repeat again to the right side, ending in right shiko dachi (not shown).

Next, slide the left foot in an arc until facing forward and, while looking 45 degrees to the right, shift your weight to the left foot and perform a right gedan sukui uke and a left ura uke simultaneously, rising into right sagi ashi dachi, hiza uchi. Follow with a right mae geri. Looking 45 degrees to the left perform the same movements from the opposite side.

After the second kick, step back into right zenkutsu dachi and strike with morote heiko tsuki, followed by left gedan tetsui into your open right hand. Cross the hands, pivot on the left foot 180 degrees and repeat to the other side (not shown). Next, perform a right ashi barai landing in heiko dachi facing 90 degrees to the right and perform a right tetsui, sukami hiki and left kagi tsuki.

Repeat the same techniques in the opposite direction. From heiko dachi, pivot 90 degrees to the left and step into right sanchin dachi. Reach out with the right hand to grab the throat and deliver a left jodan gyaku tsuki.

Slide the left foot forward and pivot 180 degrees into right neko ashi dachi and perform a swinging haito uchi, twist hands to left hip and perform mawashi uke followed by a tora guchi. Yame to finish.

THE KIHON

Kihon is relatively 'attack-and-smash' in its nature and as you move into the higher grades it becomes increasingly important to adopt the correct mindset during kihon practice. In the higher levels it is very easy for students to switch off during kihon training and lapse into a purely attack-and-smash mindset and this must be monitored and avoided at all costs.

Saifa means *'smash and tear'* and as such there is still a lot of *smash* mindset involved at this stage. In truth, the techniques to focus on during kihon are not fundamentally different to those already drilled during the Gekisai kata but it is crucial that the student's mindset is steeped in tearing free from grabs and holds during this phase of their training.

For example, when performing a low block (gedan barai) during kihon, a Gekisai student might imagine someone attacking him with a kick or a punch. The Saifa student performing exactly the same technique might imagine an attacker grabbing their wrist. While the first student would envisage blocking the strike with their gedan barai, the second would smash their blocking arm down onto their attacker's hand while ripping their grabbed hand back into the chambered position.

Similar differences might be seen for middle block (chudan uke). The Gekisai-Dai-Ichi student imagines blocking a punch. The Gekisai-Dai-Ni student imagines side-stepping and deflecting a punch. And the Saifa student imagines reaching under his grabbed hand and stripping the attacker's hold using the middle block.

Again when performing an upper block during kihon, the Gekisai-Dai-Ichi student might imagine blocking a linear face punch. The Gekisai-Dai-Ni student might imagine deflecting a jab with their covering (right) hand and blocking a haymaker with their left upper block. The Saifa student will perform

exactly the same movement but in their mind they might see someone grabbing their hair from the front. As their covering hand strikes at the crook of their attacker's arm, their upper block might smash into the wrist tearing the grip free and clearing them from the hold.

In all three of these examples the students performing the kihon would outwardly look identical. However, the actual training they are undergoing and the lessons they are learning are fundamentally different in all three cases.

This is the true beauty of kihon and the reason it is so prevalent in Karate systems. Where else can you find exactly the same movements teaching three, four, five different lessons depending on a student's grade, ability and/or understanding? Fantastic.

The Bunkai

Remember that we are exploring the area of tearing now. That said, we must not forget that the second kanji still refers to smashing so we are now starting to blend the hard with the soft, the Go with the Ju.

If we look at the first three moves of the kata we will see the same sequence repeated three times:

Clasp the right fist in the left hand and take a large step forward with the right foot. Turning the body 90 degrees to the left, bring the left foot into musubi dachi and rip the hands from the right side to the left side.

Any time something is repeated in a kata is an indicator that says *'Look at this. This is important'*, and this is no exception. The first three moves in Saifa are giving you a complete set of principles for disengaging from a hold, not just the holds indicated in the kata itself, but *any* hold.

It was never my intention for this book to list specific bunkai in detail; however, in this case the first three are rather important. So let's look at them and the principles behind them.

I.

Imagine you are facing an attacker and he reaches forward and grabs your right wrist with his left hand (what we call an 'open' grab). The dangers are headbutts and/or a right-hand punch but both are relatively unlikely given the nature of the grab. Nevertheless, the principles of positioning that you have just studied in Gekisai-Dai-Ni remain sound so you immediately step forward and to your opponent's left side. This does two things; firstly it weakens his right hand as an effective attacking weapon (albeit momentarily), and secondly, as you hold your grabbed arm tight to your body (as in the kata), it is already putting stress on the middle finger and thumb of the attacker's grabbing hand.

Holding your grabbed arm close to your body means that any twists you make with your body will be immediately transferred to your opponent's grabbing hand. Add to this the fact that you are now holding your own hand and when you simultaneously pull and twist to your left you will inevitably break free because your entire strength, power and weight is being brought to bear on his middle finger and thumb – the weakest part of his grab.

This is the key and the first principle of escape: apply force, mass and weight to the weakest part of the grabbing hand (in this case the thumb and finger).

2.

Again you are facing an attacker and he reaches forward and grabs your right wrist, this time with his right hand (what we call a 'closed' grab). You are unlikely to be struck from this position because your attacker has reached across your body and simply doesn't have the structure for a solid strike. The danger is that you will be pulled forward and across where he could easily get behind you and get your back or throat. Once again the first thing to do is move, and move forward — this time to the attacker's right (as per the kata). As before, turn in to face him as you do so. Because you have been grabbed right to right, you cannot apply

the same pressure to the finger/thumb of the grabbing hand that you did in the previous bunkai. However, your movement this time should have forced your attacker's hand into an 'S' shape. Angling your hand over the top of his wrist as you twist violently to your right will apply a pressure similar to a nikyo wrist lock, thus freeing you from the grab.

This is the second principle of escape — use body shift to put pressure on the wrist before applying force, mass and weight to the weakest part of the grabbing hand.

3.

Finally, we are back to an open grab as your attacker grabs your right wrist with his left hand. This time, as you step to his left and turn in, sweep your right hand out and over so that your right elbow comes over the top of his grabbing arm. As you drop back into shiko dachi, lever your attacker forward and down. Grab his left wrist and apply a simultaneous arm bar and wrist lock. You can either disengage or damage his elbow joint from here. Either way, the motion to apply the arm bar is still one of tearing.

This is the third principle of escape — control the body and arm before putting pressure on the wrist and applying force, mass and weight to the weakest part of the grabbing hand.

We are more concerned here with the principle than the technique and all of those listed work equally well against double-handed grabs or grabs further up the arm.

PADWORK DRILLS

In the initial stage of training the students simply walked up to the pads, got themselves nice and comfortable and began banging away. The second phase emphasised positioning, clearing, footwork, ducking, slipping and generally evading before, after and during strikes to the pads. In both of these phases the student was free to move about as they saw fit. During this third phase of training, that changes.

Saifa is all about tearing free from a grab or hold before counter-attacking with strikes, and the padwork at this stage must reflect this. As such you should be utilising scenarios where the student is initially prevented from striking the pads.

For example, have the pad-holder wear a pad on just one arm while he grabs the striker with the other. The grabbed student must tear free from his grip before striking the single pad. Use as many different forms of grab and strike sequences as you can. Alternatively, have a third student grab or pin the striker while the pad-holder stands a foot or so away. Again, it is the striker's goal to get free of the hold and attack the pads with as much violence and venom as possible.

A third example would have the student mounted on a heavy bag laid on the floor (or a fellow student if they are gloved up). On the command, the student just starts pounding the bag on the floor. After a couple of seconds have one or two more students come up and push and pull the mounted 'attacker'. His job is to ignore them totally and simply get back into position to strike the bag repeatedly. As the drill progresses, have the students clear the attacker completely from the bag. He never fights them directly; he just has to struggle free and keep hitting the bag with whatever he can and from whatever angle is available.

All of these drills are core Saifa training and this pit bull 'tear and savage' mindset is crucial at this stage of the student's development.

PARTNER DRILLS
Saifa

KAKIE

As with Gekisai-Dai-Ni, kakie should form a major part of your study of escaping. The process is the same as that described earlier although you do need to add in two more patterns.

In the Gekisai-Dai-Ni phase of training, the kakie arc was directly from sternum to sternum. Now you want to instigate a circular motion that describes a flat circle between you. In this pattern you need to be close enough that you 'receive' your partner's forward motion and you need to twist from the hips to pass it in front of your body before returning it.

Finally, you need to utilise a pattern that describes an arc in front of you from left to right. For example, you will have crossed hands with your partner and your right hand will be down to your left side, palm up. Initiating a movement not dissimilar to a dumb-bell curl, you raise up and push down to your right-hand side.

The reason we need a wider variety of patterns is because now, at random points in the kakie exercise, your partner should be grabbing you. You can be grabbed at any point of the movement and because kakie is essentially a sensitivity drill your response has to fit in as well as possible with that movement. For example, if I am grabbed as I push forwards, I must find an escape that involves me continuing that forward motion. If I am grabbed on a receiving phase, my escape must utilise this motion.

Which brings us nicely on to our next escaping exercise – throws.

THROWS (NAGE WAZA)

As with many aspects of combat, throws can be used in a number of strategic ways. Bear in mind that because we are in the 'tear-and-smash' phase of our training, throws become part of an overall strategy to break free from an attacker and get the fight back to a striking range.

The main throws indicated in Saifa are tai otoshi (body drop) and ippon seoinage (shoulder throw); however, there are also one or two early indicators of the grappling style takedowns to be studied later in Seiunchin.

Throws should, of course, be performed without the need to resort to brute strength – a big guy can, naturally, haul an untrained smaller guy over and onto the ground with relative ease. However, at its higher levels nage waza is an entirely beautiful, scientific study of body mechanics, movement and physics. In fact, the area of throwing is easily an entire lifetime of study in its own right – hence the emergence and continuation of the wonderful art of Judo.

However, as karateka we don't have a lifetime to dedicate to this one aspect of combat and so we are going to need to understand some basic principles in order to turn nage waza into a useful tool in our developing armoury.

The founder of Aikido, O Sensei Morihei Ueshiba, is quoted as having said that '90% of Aikido is atemi (striking)'. This has been subject to various interpretations over the years but as karateka, the first thing to understand about throwing is that it *must* be preceded by a strike. This might be a hard strike or it might be a soft one, but unless you are Neil Adams, some form of distraction is utterly essential to pull it off in the chaos of real combat.

The second thing to understand is the concept of breaking an opponent's balance before entering for a throw. A good way to visualise this is to imagine that you are attempting to move a wardrobe from one side of the bedroom to the other. How would you do it? Well, you could just put your shoulder to it and push, but it won't move very far — and neither will the guy you try and do this to.

The way to move that wardrobe is to get it up on one corner and 'walk' it by rocking it from side to side — from one corner to the other. Now, even here there is some subtlety to the successful manoeuvring of the wardrobe. If you pull it too much, it will fall on top of you; if you push it too much, it will fall away from you. Furthermore, if at any stage you lose control of it, it will regain its equilibrium and fall back upright.

This describes exactly what you need to do to throw someone — you need to get his weight and balance onto either his heels or his toes, depending which throw you are attempting. Ideally, your opponent should be balanced on the heel, or toes, of one foot. Sanchin is an ideal training method for this type of manipulation but that is really for another time and for now, the student basically needs to be experimenting with their own balance and with unbalancing a training partner.

MULTIPLES

Working in threes or fours, have one student in the middle while the others move around and grab his arms or wrists in turn. This must be a slow, continuous exercise with the student flowing from one escape to another. All escapes should be smooth and come about as a result of correct positioning, movement and application of weight. As soon as the student starts to try to muscle his way out, stop the exercise and start again.

This is a fantastic drill and you will notice a lot of Aikido-style movements alongside a lot of classical positioning.

SURPRISE ATTACKS

As ever in our onward progression, it's time to turn up the heat. Have two lines of students at either end of the hall. Make one student start to walk and on your signal, have one of the others run up and grab him from behind. This can be any grab — single arm, both arms, round the waist, round the neck, by the hair etc.

Once the student has freed himself have them turn around and come back. Of course, they are now attacked from the other side, again with an unspecified technique.

This is classic Saifa training and it is really where your study of the kata will be brought to life. Through these types of repeated drills, your kata will really begin to work for you as the true purpose of kata starts to come into sharp focus and the separation between kata, self-defence and fighting starts to blur.

CONDITIONING

While correct body mechanics, positioning and leverage are what is required to effectively escape a hold or grab, you won't be harmed by having strong arms and a powerful grip yourself. Chi'ishi will therefore continue to play a big role in the student's development at this stage.

Chi'ishi: In addition to technique, there are two elements which will enhance your ability to break free from a wide variety of grabs and holds — strength and flexibility. This is really where the chi'ishi comes into its own.

As well as strengthening your upper body, shoulders and chest, correct use of the chi'ishi will build genuine strength along a wide variety of moveable pathways. The almost awkward motions of the chi'ishi drills put the user's arms and wrists through a whole range of movements that will be directly used in disengagement and escape techniques. This range of movement is the real strength of the chi'ishi and there is no modern tool in the gym that does the job better.

For this reason, the chi'ishi will still form the backbone of hojo undo while the student is still in the Saifa stage of training.

In addition to the chi'ishi there are two new pieces of traditional equipment which the student should now be introduced to — the gripping jars (nigiri game), and the wrist roller (makiage kigu).

Nigiri game: These gripping jars usually have a lip at the top which can be gripped with spread fingers and hung at the side of the body. The student is required to fill the jars with ever-increasing weight (water, sand or stone as they progress) and move around holding the jars over a period of time. Students are also required to suspend the jars at arms length, to assist in developing the upper body and shoulders. The nigiri game is basically, therefore, an isometric tool. Isometric exercises involve the use of muscular contractions against a load which is fixed or immovable.

The nigiri game primarily helps to develop a strong vice-like grip. However, while use of nigiri game will undoubtedly strengthen your grip, for me, this is more about building spirit than muscle. Used in the way described, use of the nigiri game is basically putting the user into a position of stress — much like the low stances of some Karate styles — excellent for building spirit, not so useful in actual combat.

There are both benefits and drawbacks to having the muscles contract but not shorten during exercise. On the plus side, isometric exercises:

> *Develop static strength*
> *Are quick to do and don't hurt the muscles*
> *Don't need expensive equipment*
> *Can be done anywhere*

However, on the downside, isometric exercises:

> *Only produce muscle gains in strength at the precise and specific angle of the exercise*
> *Can stop the blood flow to the muscle, increase the blood pressure, and allow less blood to flow back to the heart*

Generally speaking, isometric training falls a poor second to exercises that utilise the full movement of the muscles and joints (isotonic). This form of training comes under the banner of 'resistance training'.

Resistance or isotonic exercises involve the muscles contracting and shortening across a full range of movement. The benefits of resistance training are primarily that you strengthen a muscle throughout its range of movement and you can tailor that movement to match your fighting movements.

Makiage kigu: The makiage kigu is a resistance tool and is basically a wrist roller consisting of a wooden handle with a weight hung on a rope in the centre. The user holds the wooden handle in both hands out at arm's length and twists the handle, wrapping the rope onto it and raising and lowering the weight as they do so. This is an extremely tough exercise and does an excellent job of strengthening the wrists, forearms, shoulders and grip.

In many ways the makiage kigu seeks to exercise and develop the same muscle groups as the nigiri game but in a much more dynamic and rewarding way.

This is another excellent piece of kit and you will find that nothing has superseded it over the passage of time. The fact that equipment identical to this is still found in modern gyms is testimony to its longevity, practicality and overall effectiveness.

TAMESHIWARA: TRIAL BY BREAKING

Although a karateka will never totally abandon the concept of attack-and-smash, the student has now been training in this manner for well over a year and it is time to move on. By this stage, the student should be well on their way to developing strong attacks, delivered with well-conditioned fists, and executed with power and accuracy. However, before moving on to a more grappling phase of training, there is one more trial to face: tameshiwara — trial by breaking.

In recent years tameshiwara has become something of a forgotten art. Even amongst those who haven't forgotten it, it is looked on as a bit of a relic from the past. It seems that fewer and fewer people are willing to engage in this fundamental element of Karate training. At one time tameshiwara was the standard by which a karateka was measured. It was how you tested your impact, power and courage, and it was what people expected from someone who practised Karate. In fact, tameshiwara was synonymous with Karate itself. So what went wrong?

Well, firstly there is the health issue. People became increasingly concerned that they were breaking their hands more often than they were breaking their bricks. This is true, but it's no coincidence that the increase in people getting hurt during breaking coincided with a general decrease in contact levels inside the dojo. And I'm not just talking about makiwara training here — I'm talking about general bagwork, padwork and, of course, contact sparring.

These were the tools which gradually hardened the hands of the karateka so that when the time was right, they were able to face their trial by breaking with the groundwork already done. What has changed today is that the groundwork is being overlooked. There is not enough contact in general training to harden people to the task, and when they do attempt a break they are hopelessly ill-prepared for the task and injury is the only possible outcome.

The second thing is that it takes an awful lot of work to prepare for tameshiwara. Hours and hours need to be spent on the bag and on the makiwara. And the reason that it needs be hours and hours is that in order to do it safely, it must be done gradually over a long period of time. Generally speaking, people are simply not prepared to put that level of long-term training in any more.

Even those wishing to break seem to be content to spend a few months on the makiwara, before wheeling out the boards/brick/tiles etc. Again, injury is the only possible outcome.

The third thing that happened was the use of tameshiwara as a demonstration tool. Don't get me wrong, I love to see breaking at a Karate event. I have early and lasting memories of seeing Mick Lambert, Kim Roberts and Dave Arnold smashing through all manner of construction materials and it was one of the first things that drew me to Karate in the first place. But, because it became so high profile, out came the charlatans. This is where you hear tales of people baking bricks, sawing through boards, gluing boards together and so on. Now you may be thinking, sure, but it's just a demonstration — so what?

Well, the so what is the people watching the demonstration. They are not to know that it's faked so they witness incredible feats of breaking and, human nature being what it is, sooner or later someone will try to emulate that break — only for real. Any guesses on the outcome? It's a bit like bringing our children up watching Bruce Willis getting smashed over the head with chairs and bottles with no ill effect, only to be surprised when one kid stoves another's head in with a chair or a bottle. Needless to say, unlike in the movies, this time the victim doesn't just shake it off, and we are left with two victims — the one who got hit and the one we educated to think that everything would be okay.

There are people who have never even attempted to break a brick who will tell you that it is easy. Let me just put that one straight. Breaking a house brick with your bare hands is no easy task. It takes skill, speed, focus, power and, yes, it takes conditioning.

Things change in the martial arts. Exercises that were commonplace in the 1970s have now, quite rightly, been consigned to the scrapheap. But with regards to tameshiwara, I think we are once again in danger of throwing the baby out with the bath water. Conditioning is a fundamental part of Karate — like it or not. Having fists hardened enough to deliver bone-crushing blows is part and parcel of being a karateka. It might not be the most sophisticated expression of our art form, but it is, nonetheless, a fundamental part of being a karateka.

To be honest, I blame Bruce Lee. His 'boards don't hit back' comment has allowed countless potentially genuine karateka to devalue and opt out of this crucial element of their training — if Bruce Lee said it, it must be true! It is true that boards don't hit back, but then nor do focus mitts, Thai pads, heavy bags, wooden dummies, speed balls, or any number of other training aids. Actually, to be fair to Bruce, it was only ever said in a movie, but Lee and movies are so intrinsically linked that it is very difficult to separate the man from the movie star.

So what is the true nature and goal of tameshiwara? As mentioned in the title of this section, tameshiwara literally means *trial by breaking*. And it is exactly that. It is a trial, an ordeal that a student must face as he makes his way along the path. In this context it is not a test of speed, strength or power (although these things are useful); it is a test of courage.

For tameshiwara to work as the invaluable training aid that I have found it to be, four key elements must be in place:

> The student must know a long time ahead that at some point he will be called upon to break
> The Sensei must guide and prepare that student so that he is ready for the test both mentally and physically
> The student must not be allowed to practise breaking prior to the test
> The break must be public

Let's take a look at each of these elements in turn to see how they all fit together.

Firstly, the student must know a long time ahead that at some point he will be called upon to break. As with any trial, most of the battle is mental. In Goju, the first break is done at the end of the green belt grading. This is deemed to be the first level of strength and is a tough grading to get through. Beginners who watch the grading and the break see what will be expected of them further down the line, should they decide to continue along the path. In this way they can begin to prepare for what will need to be done.

Secondly, the Sensei must guide and prepare that student so that he is ready for the test both mentally and physically. It is the job of the teacher to ensure that students have access to all the training and information that they need to attempt, and pass, the grades and tests set in front of them. Tameshiwara doesn't need to be openly discussed as long as the teacher ensures that sufficient (and gradual) conditioning is taking place.

Use of pads, heavy bags, contact sparring etc. all need to be working towards a common goal. The three gradings prior to green belt also need to be working towards the physical and mental hardening of the individual. That is the teacher's job and how a student approaches his first break is not only a test of the student's courage, but of the Sensei's methods.

Thirdly, the student must not be allowed to practise breaking prior to the test. It is perfectly understandable for anyone who has a test to perform to wish to practise it beforehand. In most circumstances, this is a good thing; in the case of tameshiwara, it shows a misunderstanding of the concept.

Practice allows students to gauge whether or not they can complete a task. This reduces stress which in turn reduces fear. But remember that tameshiwara is a trial, and this trial uses fear as its most potent ingredient. The first time a student breaks should be on the day of the test. That's what turns it into a test of courage.

The fear isn't just there to be conquered; it's there to be used. When a student faces that one inch thick, solid wooden board for the first time, he is riddled with doubt. That doubt creates fear which in turn releases adrenalin. And it is that adrenalin which will ultimately help the student to power through that break. Anyone who has worked on the doors or front-line security for any length of time learns to use this adrenalin drop to their own ends. The structured approach to tameshiwara begins to teach this invaluable lesson in a manner that is very difficult to replicate in any other way.

Finally, the break must be public. When I was coming up through the kyu grades in the late 1970s and early 1980s, it was commonplace for black belt gradings to be done behind closed doors. This kept an air of mystery around the higher level gradings, and while this in itself served to generate a certain degree of fear, it only lasted until the student began the test and realised that in truth, it was all very familiar.

It wasn't until I met Sensei Nick Hughes of Combat Karate and Fight Survival Training (F.I.S.T.) that I began to change my outlook on this. Nick, a veteran of the French Foreign Legion and no stranger to fear and its uses, advocated the use of public gradings. In fact, he went so far as to personally invite a candidate's family, friends and all local martial artists to attend. The reason he did this was that, far from making this a more relaxed environment to test under, it served to pile on the pressure.

If gradings are about anything at all, they are about performing under pressure. I mentioned that the first time a student breaks it should be at the test. Added to all that uncertainty and self-doubt is the fact that all his friends and fellow karateka are watching him, and you can begin to see the nature of the trial.

Karate isn't about turning up to training twice a week; it's about overcoming obstacles and facing fears. Once a student enters a Karate dojo they must be prepared to face fear and it is our job as instructors not only to provide those obstacles and trials, but to make sure that the students have developed the physical and mental attributes to equip them for the coming challenges.

The greater the effort, the greater the reward, and the physical and symbolic effects of a student breaking through his first ever tameshiwara is a prize we should be very loath to lose.

THE NEXT STAGE

So, how has our young student developed as a fighter?

Remember that we took someone who had no concept of how to fight and ingrained in them the simple but effective concept of a direct, blitzing attack-and-smash strategy.

Once this was well ingrained we started to move the fight closer. The closer range dictated the need for a more sophisticated strategy and our student was refined to incorporate movement, evasion, redirection and positioning before unleashing the direct assault.

Once our student was more or less comfortable at these ranges, it was time to move the fight closer still. No longer in the area of fisticuffs, the student now found himself being grabbed and held. At this stage, his basic fight strategy remained relatively unchanged and the primary goal once grabbed, was to break free and get the fight back to the attack-and-smash range and strategy that has become his staple diet over the last couple of years or so.

There is one final step to be taken before our karateka can be deemed to be versed in all ranges of combat. We need to move the fight into the final possible range: close-quarter-combat grappling.

It is now time for Seiunchin — trapping battle.

CHAPTER 11
TRAPPING BATTLE
(SEIUNCHIN)

The Principle: *Suppress and control*
The Mindset: *Submit, break or render unconscious*
The Area of Combat: *Close-quarter grappling*

Man, it's cold tonight. It's nearly two in the morning and I've been stood on this door since seven. Still, another half-hour and it's home, bed, sleep. Mind you, it looks like Big Neil's half asleep already. It's been a long night but nothing out of the ordinary. We've stopped two stag parties from coming in, removed one lad for being sick in the toilets and thrown two guys out for hassling some of the girls — pretty normal night all told. Okay, that's about the last of them. I'll just go out and check the fire doors then we're done for the night. I walk round the corner and try all the doors — everything is fine. As I turn to head back in, there's a blinding flash and everything goes dark for a second. My vision clears to see one of the guys we threw out earlier standing in front of me. I grab him by the shirt, ready to bang him up against the wall when there is a second flash and I drop to my knees. I'm cursing myself for being so stupid. I've been set up and the second guy has just sucker punched me from the side. I know I'm going down but I have the presence of mind to pull the first guy down with me. I try to push him in the way of the kicks now flying in from the lowlife who just dropped me. There's a thud and a scuffle kicks off above me as Big Neil piles in to help. It's now one-on-one. I'm underneath and my attacker is raining punches down but I wrap him up, roll him over and choke him out. I get up to help Neil but he doesn't need my help and there's only the two of us left standing in the car park. Not so cold now, is it? Still, we're done here. Home, bed, sleep...

PRINCIPLES OF SEIUNCHIN

Seiunchin consists of two primary concepts, *'seiun'* meaning 'trapping/control', and *'chin'*, meaning 'battle'. Literally, therefore, Seiunchin translates as 'trapping battle' and is basically a grappling kata emphasising close-quarter fighting techniques.

Up to this point we have more or less kept the fight at arm's length. Even when the Saifa concepts of grabbing and pulling were introduced, the fight strategy was to tear free, rip away and get back to a stand-up impact range. The concepts of trapping and control can only really mean one thing – the fight has moved even closer and our area of study for the following year or so is grappling.

Grappling really comes about when two combatants become locked together during the chaos of a fight.

This can either be standing up, in a clinch, or rolling around on the floor. The position doesn't actually matter; the principles outlined in Seiunchin remain true for both scenarios.

One of the main differences between the grappling you see in something like MMA and the ground-fighting you might encounter on the street is that in MMA at least one of the parties usually wants the fight to end up on the floor. In the outside world, no one in their right mind would deliberately take a fight to the ground.

When I was growing up as a kid in Belfast, only girls kicked. The guys would knock each other senseless, but they wouldn't kick somebody when they were down. Shoot them, possibly. Kick them, no way. But times have changed.

If you hit the floor nowadays, not only will all your attacker's mates pile in, but even passers-by might have a punt at you. Regardless of your level of grappling skills, your primary goal once you hit the floor should be to get to your feet as soon as possible.

We are martial artists and the way we train is to prepare for the worst-case scenario. Believe me, hitting the ground is often the worst-case scenario, so you need to know how to deal with it.

In 'self-defence' terms, a Saifa-type fight-to-escape approach is still probably your best bet. However, the skills required to break free from someone are a world away from the skills required to deliberately *not* break away from him — the skills required to control, manoeuvre and ultimately submit him, break him,

or render him unconscious, will take you to a new level entirely. These skills are extremely high-level, requiring a deep understanding of movement and balance; an in-depth understanding of muscular and skeletal structures; and, above all, a highly developed feel for sensitivity.

As mentioned previously, the fact that it is far easier to represent a striking technique within a kata than it is to represent a grappling one has led many people to assume that there is no grappling within the kata. This is, of course, a big mistake and Seiunchin is specifically designed to give you the skills you need when it all goes pear-shaped and you find yourself up-close and personal.

GROUND-FIGHTING IN CONTEXT
The fall and rise of grappling

When the newly named system of Karate was exported to mainland Japan from the Okinawan prefecture it was eager to be recognised as an 'official' martial art. Unfortunately for Karate, this meant finding a niche that was not already filled. Ju-jitsu was already dealing with close-quarter combat. Judo had specialised in the purity of throws and grappling. Aikido was the art of harmony. What was left? There was room for an art that specialised in punching and kicking.

In Okinawa, training had been relatively informal – many classes were held in the teacher's back garden. Training outdoors on the ground allowed practitioners to practise throws, take-downs and grappling techniques with full power. However, in Japan, Karate became more official. Class sizes grew as Karate entered the Japanese consciousness and, more importantly, the Japanese university system. Training took place in recognised dojos on hardwood floors, where, with the best will in the world, full power throws and ground-fighting cannot be practised properly. If you are training indoors, mats are every bit as much a training aid as pads or kick shields – allowing you to perform with a far higher level of power and impact.

I was once told that you can tell what a chief instructor is good at by looking at his syllabus. There is much truth in this simple statement, and I fear we are all guilty. I am a firm believer in the grading system and I have witnessed its benefits repeatedly over the years, but it does have drawbacks too. It is very difficult for a high-grade to stand at the front of a class of thirty people and teach something that they are not particularly good at. The reason is that constant demon of the martial artist – ego.

The same situation would not be a problem in the honest environment of a boxing gym, There, the coach isn't expected to be better than his fighters at the physical aspects of his discipline – he is just

expected to know more. The same cannot be said of martial arts, so a particularly negative cycle begins: teachers who can't kick very well don't teach a lot of kicking and so their students can't kick very well either. Teachers whose kata performance isn't particularly strong might choose to emphasise kumite, and so will their students, when their time comes to teach. Once an element such as ground-fighting starts to slip, it only takes one generation before it is lost.

This negative cycle has been a major cause of the catastrophic omission of grappling in a great many Karate schools over the last hundred years or so. Fortunately, in the form of the kata, we still retain the original records – so those willing to look, and able to interpret the codes, can piece the original systems together again in their intended forms.

Ground-fighting is, and always has been, an integral part of Okinawan Goju Ryu – just as it was for other early Karate systems. In fact, being able to fight on the ground is an essential element of any discipline that claims to be a fighting system. Of course, different systems specialise in different areas of combat, but it is simply not enough to focus solely on one area. This was demonstrated most eloquently in the early 1990s in the Octagon of the UFC and, in many ways, MMA is actually a revivalist movement (albeit in the form of a combat sport) and has actually returned to the original core of many fighting systems.

Amongst many things, the early MMA scene served to showcase the skills of competent grapplers in dealing with stand-up fighters. In the ring or cage, the grapplers repeatedly took the strikers down and submitted them. This sent shockwaves through the martial arts community and undoubtedly did a lot of good for martial arts in general. However, it also led to some rather bizarre claims about the number of 'streetfights' that end up on the ground – the statistics varied, but figures as high as 90% were quoted. While it's vital that you achieve competence on the ground, it is also important to realise that this figure is nonsense.

Over the years, I have fought in semi-contact and full-contact stand-up matches where grappling was not allowed. I have fought in grappling bouts where strikes were not allowed, and I have fought in limited/no-rules bouts where almost anything was allowed. Outside the dojo I worked on the doors of pubs and clubs for many years. I have taught courses to the police and the military as well as teaching door supervisor courses to bouncers in pubs and clubs around the UK. I make these statements to demonstrate that, while my experience is by no means all-encompassing, I have been involved with violence and violent confrontations enough to make some reasonably sound observations on the way these things work. And I would like to categorically observe that 90% of fights do *not* go to the ground. In fact, in my experience, nothing like 9 in 10 fights get anywhere *near* the ground. So where did this statistic come from?

In the late 1990s, the Los Angeles Police Department was charged with finding out how to better prepare law enforcement officers for violent confrontations. When their findings were published in the Los Angeles Times Magazine in 1998, they included the statement that *'...a substantial number of arrests that involved force could have been prevented or handled better if the officers had been more well-trained'* The basis for this conclusion was apparently that 62% of all altercations had taken place with both parties on the ground, a situation which the officers in the LAPD had not anticipated or trained for.

We, therefore, have a verified, legitimate study showing 6 in 10 altercations ending up on the ground. But there's a problem. It's not really a fight – or at least only one party is 'fighting'.

The police are charged with 'restraining' a suspect, so they are often forced to take a struggling suspect to the ground in order to subdue him. What they are strictly not allowed to do is fight in a manner which would truly represent fighting – kicks, punches, elbows, headbutts etc. Under these circumstances it's perfectly understandable that a high number of incidents go to the ground. But law enforcement is a specialist area. What about fights in pubs and clubs?

In 15 years of doorwork, I could probably count the number of times I've gone to ground with a customer on the fingers of one hand. I have worked with some doormen over the years who have *never* gone to the ground. Think back to any altercations you have witnessed involving customers and doormen and I'll bet 9 in 10 were not on the floor.

Which brings us to the next possibility – punter on punter. This is where fights do tend to end up on the floor on a fairly regular basis. Two untrained, unskilled, drunken fools flailing around like windmills do indeed tend to bump into each other eventually and fall over. However, this is largely down to incompetence. Things are likely to be very different for a skilled stand-up fighter.

The only area where I have managed to find any supporting evidence for the 90% claim has been in the area of male on female attack. Attacks on women are often sexually motivated and in these situations, going to the ground is a direct result of the nature of the assault. But again, this type of attack is not what people usually mean when they talk about a 'fight'.

Simply put, 90% of fights do not go to the ground and I have yet to meet anybody directly involved with security or conflict resolution who agrees with this 90% figure.

It is therefore crucial that you do not overweight the likelihood of having to grapple on the floor within your overall training regime. Having said that, it is equally vital that you understand that a fight is subject to chaos and despite what you want or plan for, some fights *will* end up on the floor. A martial artist needs to be prepared for the worst and, since you are training to become the complete, well-rounded fighter that Karate meant you to be, you need to become proficient on the ground.

Position, control, technique: There is a common perception among those less well versed in ground-fighting that biting and gouging are the answer to all grappling problems. While biting and gouging are indeed core Karate weapons, to cite them as an effective counter to all grappling techniques is simply naive.

First, there are times when you need to subdue somebody rather than damage him. You might be working in security, the police force, the prison service or on a hospital ward. You might find yourself fighting someone you know. I have a very close friend who is totally unable to drink whiskey. In the past I have walked into a pub and seen him on his own at the bar (that should have warned me from the start). I've gone up to him to say hello and BANG – he's punched me straight in the face. He is a lovely guy but with a few drinks inside him he doesn't even know who I am. There is no way I'm going to hurt him, but equally, I'm not having him hurt me either. Subduing him is the only option, and let me tell you, it's a sight harder than knocking him out.

The second problem is one of mimicry. Have you ever watched a sparring match that has gone on for a while before someone throws a kick? However, once that first kick is thrown, it is immediately answered with a kick from the other side. The reason for this is people get locked into modes and patterns of fighting, but once that pattern is broken, they are apt to think *'hey, that's a good idea'*, and reply in kind. So if you are on the ground, and decide to bite someone, you sure as hell better be in a superior position of control. If not, you have just given him the idea and he will pin you down and tear chunks out of you.

Biting is a massively efficient tool but to use it effectively, it needs to follow exactly the same progression as any other technique – position, control, technique. Without gaining a good position, you will never gain control of your opponent. Without gaining control of your opponent, you will never be able to apply a decent technique.

So, even if biting, gouging and scratching is your grappling fight strategy, and I can think of a lot worse, you still need to practise grappling skills in order to put yourself in a position to be able to bring these weapons effectively to bear.

The Kata: *Seiunchin*

Slide into right naname shiko dachi (45 degrees) and execute yama uke whilst keeping the eyes to the front. Rotate the hands from the wrists bringing first the back of the fingers, then the back of the hands and finally the forearms together. Hands are now open palm up at neck level. Pull both hands into fists and execute morote gedan barai slowly. Perform right ura uke and right hike uke, pulling the opponent into left nukite at belt level. Slide into left 45-degree shiko dachi and repeat (not shown). Slide into right 45-degree shiko dachi and repeat for the third time (not shown).

Place your right fist in your upturned left hand. Pulling up, perform right kakato geri followed by right soe tsuki in right sanchin dachi. Step back into left sanchin executing right shiro empi uchi followed by right mae empi uchi into your left hand. Stepping 45 degrees to the right, perform right soe uke in right sanchin dachi. Step forward into left shiko dachi, then left gedan barai. Step back 180 degrees into right shiko dachi, then right gedan barai. Step forward and perform left soe uke in left sanchin dachi. Step forward into right shiko dachi, then right gedan barai. Step back into left shiko dachi, then left gedan barai (not shown).

Step back into right shiko dachi and perform hara uke. Step back into left shiko dachi and perform hara uke again. Step forward into right sanchin dachi and execute right mawashi ude uchi into left hand quickly followed by right uraken uchi. Step right foot across to face 45 degrees to the rear in left sanchin dachi and perform jogi uke.

Perform right naname fumikomi geri into right shiko dachi followed by right age tsuki, right uraken uchi and right gedan barai.
Step back into left shiko dachi, then left gedan barai to the rear.

Pull up into right neko ashi dachi facing the front. Bring the open hands together, left on right, up to your chest and in front of your face whilst rising in your stance. Closing the fists, drop your weight back down while performing left shiro empi uchi and right mae empi uchi simultaneously. As you do so throw your hips and head back as you drop back into neko ashi dachi. Step back into left neko ashi dachi and repeat.

Step left foot across to face 45 degrees to the rear in right sanchin dachi and repeat the entire sequence the other way. Step forward into right sanchin dachi blocking left osae uke to the solar plexus and striking right uraken uchi. Step back into left neko ashi dachi and perform yama uke. Yame to finish.

In your early Karate training, you are often told to imagine that you are fighting an opponent when you perform a kata. This is absolutely correct and with a primarily striking kata, such as Gekisai-Dai-Ichi, the mindset of the students should indeed be on the imaginary opponent in front of them. However, as with much of what you are taught in the early stages of anything, this is a somewhat simplistic approach.

In truth, all students have to go through two main stages when attempting to learn a new kata. Initially, when they are still struggling to remember the moves, they are totally focused on their own bodies – which hand blocks first, which foot goes where etc. Later on, when the physical pattern is suitably ingrained, they start to think outside themselves – visualising the destruction of an imaginary attacker. However, in the higher levels, there is also a third stage, and as is often the way in the martial arts, it is cyclical and the student once again finds themselves focused inwards on the internal workings of their own bodies.

With a grappling kata such as Seiunchin, this internalisation is more readily apparent and the student should be focusing on their own musculature when performing the kata rather than extending their attention outwards towards an imaginary opponent.

So, for example, if you take the first move of Seiunchin where the student slides into shiko dachi and performs yama uke, you will often see the move performed with the back rigidly straight, the shoulders back, and the chest puffed out. This is generally done for aesthetic reasons. There are very few fighting situations which would utilise such a vulnerable position and the shoulders should be forward. Bear in mind that in shiko dachi we are either picking someone up or dragging someone down and this move is much more akin to a wrestler's crouch than something you might see on an army parade ground.

The principle of looking inward should permeate all kihon at this stage and the students should be forced to evaluate and re-evaluate their own structure as they progress through whatever series of kihon moves you are setting them. Heavy use should be made of low shiko dachi in the moving basics (kihon ido) and the students should focus heavily on the vertical power lines associated with such a low stance.

The Bunkai

Once again, the bunkai must follow the guiding principles of the area of combat associated with your current kata. In the case of Seiunchin, trapping battle, all your 'battles' must involve trapping and be restrictive in nature.

Also bear in mind that a low stance often indicates a ground technique, or at least techniques applicable for both stand-up and the ground. So, for example, let's look again at the opening sequence of Seiunchin where the student slides into shiko dachi and performs yama uke. There are clearly a number of techniques designed specifically for grabs while standing, and a number of techniques of specific use on the floor.

Standing Technique for Yama Uke

An attacker grabs both of your wrists. Drive your right hand up between his arms and bring your right elbow down on the outside of his right elbow. This will spin him slightly to his right allowing you to move behind him and take his eyes from behind. Drop into shiko dachi (and yama uke) to take the man down.

GROUND TECHNIQUE FOR YAMA UKE

You have hit the ground and in the chaos of the struggle have ended up on top but in your attacker's guard (soko shihai) i.e. your opponent is on his back but you are trapped between his legs. This is not an ideal position for your attacker but, because he has his legs around your waist, it does mean that he can control your hips and hence your balance. If he knows what he is doing he can avoid your punches and even take control from this position so it is important that you are able to escape from here.

In fact, escaping from the guard is one of the first things that a new student in MMA will be taught and it is no coincidence that it is the very first move of our very first grappling kata.

Sit up and establish as solid a base as you can (this solid base is what the shiko dachi was alluding to). From this position perform yama uke, driving your elbows into the nerves on the inside of your attacker's thighs, forcing him to release his grip and enabling you to pass his guard and obtain a more advantageous position.

If we move a little further on in the kata we come to the assisted block (soe uke) where the right hand appears to perform a middle block with the left hand supporting the right fist. As with the yama uke, we can again see techniques applicable to vertical and horizontal fighting positions.

STANDING TECHNIQUE FOR SOE UKE

An attacker swings a right-hand haymaker punch at
your head. Cover and block with your right forearm
(soto uke) and immediately ricochet your right elbow
into the right side of his head. Keeping your elbow in
contact with his head, snake your right arm around
his neck, pulling him forwards and ending up with
his head under your arm and your forearm across his
jaw. Place your assisting (left) hand under your right
fist and lever up to apply a neck crank.

GROUND TECHNIQUE FOR SOE UKE

Again you have hit the ground, only this time in the chaos of the struggle you have ended up underneath with your attacker in your guard. This is a bad position for you but you need to maintain control of your opponent via your guard. It is at this point that a ring sport diverges from the reality of a street conflict – you cannot afford to simply hold your attacker in your guard. He is likely to have mates so you need to get this over with and, in any case, sooner or later you are going to have to let him go, so you need to be able to end the fight from this position.

Again, Seiunchin has some pointers as to how this might be done. If your attacker places his right hand on the floor to your left-hand side (or you force his hand to that position), take hold of his right wrist with your left hand. Sit up and pass your right arm high over his right arm. Snake your right arm behind his head and around his neck. Bring the supporting hand into play and while controlling his hips lean back to apply a guillotine choke.

Seiunchin is littered with these dual applications and it is in this spirit that the kata should be studied and investigated.

PADWORK DRILLS

Many people hold the mistaken impression that you cannot use pads in a grappling context but this is simply untrue. Remember that although we are learning wrestling type skills, we are karateka and we are not trying to become wrestlers. Strikes are always going to be utilised, no matter what range we find ourselves in.

So, padwork at this level should concentrate on combining punches and strikes with grappling-type take-downs. For example, you might use a left–right punching combination to set up a double leg shoot/take-down (as seen in Saifa kata). Key here is timing and making sure that you end up on top following the take-down.

Similarly, you might perform a right–left punch combination on the pads, followed by a right inner thigh kick, opening your opponent up for a hip throw (o-goshi). The pads here are being used to set up as wide a variety of throws or take-downs as you can possibly train.

The second area you should be focusing on at this level is striking from the ground. This should be done from the top position, from the bottom position, from the side position – in fact, from as many awkward and difficult positions as you can put yourself and your partner into.

As an example of a groundwork-type pad drill try the following:

Start from a standing position and set up a left–right punch combination followed by a double leg shoot/take-down. Get into your partner's guard and perform ten rapid punches on the pads. Use yama uke to escape the guard and move into side position (yoko shihai). Perform ten rapid punches on the pads from this awkward position. Move over into the full mount (kami shihai) and again deliver ten rapid punches on the pads.

Have your partner roll you over so you are now mounted and again perform ten rapid punches from your back.

Delivering power from these awkward positions is a real challenge and is, again, one which the kata set out to address. In the West, punching power tends to come from the rotation of the shoulder girdle. This allows for a huge amount of rotational power and hence impact. However, what happens when the ability to rotate is removed – when you find yourself on the ground for example? Well, basically you have to use other mechanisms in order to source power. This is why so many kata start with a double block and then punch while leaving one hand in the blocking position. This effectively eliminates any potential for upper body rotation and puts you into worst-case scenario punching territory. Sanchin kata deals very heavily with this worst-case scenario power sourcing.

Performing pad drills in the format suggested above not only serves to enhance the student's punching ability in restricted spaces, it also helps to ensure that they do not fall totally into the 'grappling trap' where fighters switch totally from one mode to the other, completely forgetting to grapple when they are striking, or completely forgetting to strike while they are grappling.

PARTNER DRILLS
Seiunchin

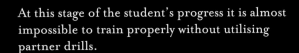

At this stage of the student's progress it is almost impossible to train properly without utilising partner drills.

Previous work via kakie will have laid much of the groundwork with regards to developing the sensitivity needed once the fight gets up close. At this range, sight is no longer your primary sense and touch takes over.

In fact, when attempting to assess whether or not a system originally included grappling, a primary indicator is the presence of sensitivity drills or specific tools for developing touch sensitivity. Many (not all) of the Japanese systems lack these drills. Many (not all) of the old Okinawan systems include them. And in truth, you would be hard pushed to find any of the old style Chinese Kung Fu systems which did not contain at least some element of sensitivity training. Despite what some people would have you think, it is this heightened awareness of sensitivity which actually turns something like Tai Chi into a genuinely viable fighting art.

Kakie: Of course, kakie should be worked heavily at this stage with the main focus being on unbalancing and redirecting force into either throws or grappling take-downs.

During this phase of training it is important to maintain the clear distinction in mindset between the Saifa and Seiunchin approaches. In Saifa, the range has closed and you really don't want to be there — your goal is to escape. In Seiunchin, the range has closed but you *do* want to be there; you might even have initiated the closeness — your goal here is to deal with the situation from where you are, i.e. not to escape.

As such, kakie training should now focus on finding the timing and opening for closing in on your partner. As you will soon discover, if you move in too soon your movement will easily be blocked or countered.

If you move in too late, you will be an easy target for punches, elbows or knee strikes. Something worth getting right, I'm sure you agree.

Randori: Randori is one of those words that different people use to mean different things. In this case I am referring to free-form stand-up interplay. There are, of course, numerous drills, patterns and exercises from this position and you should design, develop, seek out and experiment with as many of them as possible. However, here are a couple that I have found extremely useful over the years.

a) Fighting for position: Start clinched together with one arm over your partner's shoulder, and your other arm tucked under his arm. The goal here is to get both of your arms under both of his. In order to achieve this you need to take your arm off his shoulder and feed it in under his other arm. Of course, by the time you have done this, he has done the same to you on the other side so you are back to square one and off you go again. Although simple, this is an exhausting drill and extremely good for focusing the mind on the 'position first' mindset.

Although this is also true of stand-up fighting, the need to establish a good position before launching an attack is brought into very sharp focus once the fight hits the floor. In fact, the single biggest mistake that beginners make on the ground is to try to apply chokes, locks and strangles before they have established a good solid positional advantage. All this early attack does is show your opponent what you are doing and gives them ample time to escape. It's far better to manipulate your opponent into a position where, once the technique is applied, they have nowhere to go and no choice but to either tap out or pass out.

b) Throws and take-downs: Start with your right hand holding your partner's left lapel and your left hand holding your partner's right sleeve. Have him do the same. As you move around, the goal here is to take down or throw your partner to the floor. This is very similar to a traditional Judo bout, although as the student progresses you should add in short-range strikes and blows in order to soften up and aid the throw.

Of course, all throws should be considered legitimate in this exercise but in terms of where you start, you should probably focus on one major hip throw (e.g. o-goshi), one major shoulder throw (e.g. ippon seionage), one major leg throw (e.g. tai otoshi) and one major leg reap (e.g. osoto gari). All other variations can be added over time.

Cooperative grappling: With the possible exception of free-grappling, this is probably the single most useful exercise you can find on the floor.

Of course, at this phase of the student's training he will be being taught the basics of strangles, locks and chokes – i.e. the 'tools' for submission grappling. It is not my intention to cover exactly how to perform these techniques here and, for the purposes of this exercise, I am making the assumption that the student either knows these techniques or, again, has easy access to the required knowledge.

Have both students go to the floor and specify one single technique that they want to work on – for example, choose a specific arm bar or strangle. Have the students roll around in the manner of a free fight but only one of them is attempting to apply the technique. The other is merely moving in the style of a fight and presenting 'opportunities' for the arm bar. Make it clear that this is 'cooperative' and the students are only fighting/resisting at around 30% – 40%. This figure can be increased as the skills develop.

The goal here is for the student to apply the chosen technique from as many positions as possible – on top, underneath and from either side.

You can let this run with the same student performing the same technique (from different positions) over and over. You can let them go turn for turn using the same technique. Or you can give them each a different technique to perform. The key is that the students cooperate with each other, and that they only work one technique at a time.

CONDITIONING

As with all things in the martial arts, conditioning is a long-term process and it is important to understand that moving on to another phase of training is done *in addition to* the previous work, *not instead of*. As such, the student should still be working the chi'ishi, makiwara, nigiri game, and makiage kigu. The big addition and primary tool of hojo undo at this stage of the syllabus is the kongoken; the 'iron ring'.

In Karate terms the kongoken is fairly specific to Okinawan Goju Ryu and is basically a result of Goju's greater emphasis on grappling and groundwork. Goju founder Chojun Miyagi Sensei (himself a grappler of some note) fashioned the kongoken after fighting and training with wrestlers in Hawaii where a similar piece of equipment is still used to this day.

The shape and weight of a kongoken (usually a six-foot oval ring weighing upward of 70 pounds) makes it a very useful tool in the development of a strong body and is particularly useful for developing powerful grappling techniques. It covers a wide variety of exercises such as squats, bench press, military press, twists etc., that can be used to develop power in the shoulders, hips and legs. It also helps with the strength and coordination required to perform throwing techniques.

While many of these exercises can be performed perfectly well in a modern gym, what the kongoken does very well is allow you access to a very wide variety of solid composite strengthening exercises via one simple piece of equipment – fantastic if you have no access to a full gym and/or no mates...

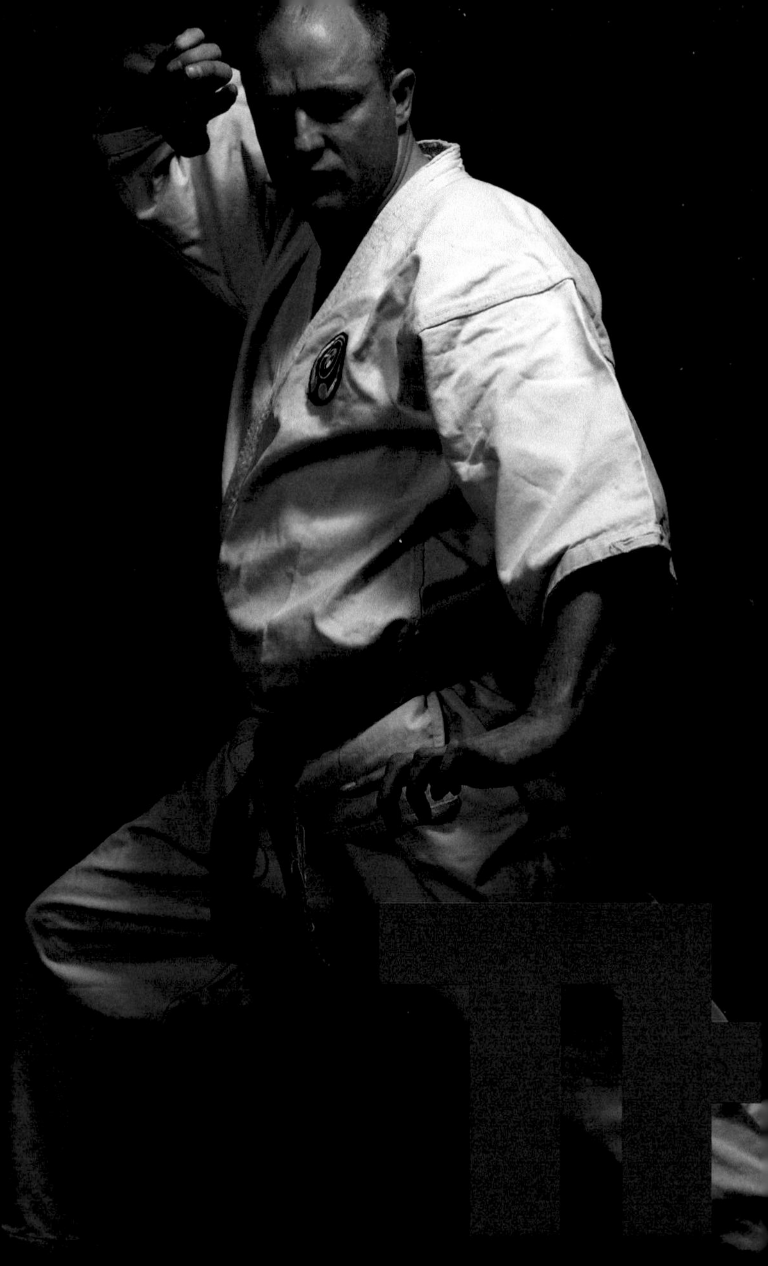

PART 4 END?

Black Belt
The End or the Beginning?

When we first met our troubled young student he had no concept of how to fight. He does now. We got to work immediately and ingrained in him a simple but highly effective fight strategy — the direct, blitzing attack-and-smash.

Once this was second nature to him, we moved the fight closer. The closer range dictated the need for a more sophisticated strategy and our student was forced to refine his tactics to incorporate movement, evasion, redirection and positioning before unleashing his direct attack-and-smash assault.

As our student started to get comfortable again (a big no-no in martial arts) we once again moved him out of his comfort zone and pulled the fight in closer still. No longer in familiar territory, the student found himself being pushed, pulled, grabbed and held. At this stage, his basic fight strategy remained relatively unchanged and his primary goal was to break free and get the fight back to his familiar attack-and-smash range.

Finally, when being grabbed no longer held any particular fear for our student, we finished the picture and moved the fight into the final range — close-quarter grappling combat. Through a clearly defined and laid-out training programme (all outlined in the kata), we have gradually and progressively hardened the mind, body and spirit of a young man who initially came to us for that very purpose.

But, most importantly of all, we have taken somebody who had been picked on, humiliated and victimised and shown him that it doesn't have to be like that — there is a different way. The way of the martial arts.

We have come a long way since that frightened, beat-up little kid shuffled self-consciously into our dojo. Five years or more have passed and that 'little kid' is now a fully fledged Karate black belt.

When our student first set out on his martial arts journey, the black belt was simply an unobtainable goal — a goal so far out of his reach that even the possibility seemed ridiculous. And now, five years and four shades on, here he is. Goal achieved. Dream realised. Destination reached. So, how does it feel?

Well, to be perfectly honest, it feels weird. Empty. Maybe even phoney. Either way, it definitely feels like an anticlimax, at least for a while. You see, even though he had been told a thousand times, deep down, he still really wanted to believe that a black belt was an 'expert'. The realisation that this is really not the case takes a while to settle in.

What had been seen for so long as a final destination has turned out to be nothing of the sort. It's not a final destination at all; it's simply a gateway to a whole new world. The black belt indicates a graduation to a new beginning. He may have covered the basics, but he has a whole world of learning ahead of him. As this fact washes over him, the disappointment fades and a whole new wave of excitement hits him. The martial arts path was once seen as a daunting single-track route from white to black. But now, from the staging post of the black belt, the enormity of the martial possibilities just seems endless. There are no styles — only a variety of maps and guides around different areas of the same territory. So much more to study. So much more to learn. So much more to perfect. Beautiful.

We have followed a well-trodden but perhaps, in recent times, somewhat overgrown and less used path to develop a fighter who is familiar, well versed and competent in all ranges of fighting. Karate was never just about punching and kicking. Kata was never simply about perfecting movement. Karate was, and remains, a total fighting system. Over the years this simple truth appears to have been forgotten, buried or hidden, but deep down, a great many karateka have kept the faith. Many have continued with their art, knowing that elements appeared to be missing and yet confident that ultimately their chosen art would deliver and that its secrets would be revealed. Well, as is often the case with 'secrets', this whole training map was right in front of us all the time — 'hidden' within the system of kata bequeathed to us by the masters all those years ago.

The 'secret' of kata is that the richness and depth lies not within our perfection of the movements themselves, nor within how many techniques we can pull out of a kata, but within our overall understanding, training and development within the *spirit* of the kata itself.

THE FINAL CONFLICT

The local is crowded tonight and today's game is being replayed on the big screen. Ordinarily I avoid the pub on these nights but tonight I just fancied a pint. Thought I'd nip out and see if there are any friendly faces around for a chat and a beer. As it happens, I don't know anyone in here — some local. After waiting far too long I've eventually been served and I spot a free table over by the back, away from the telly, and start to weave my way through the mass of red shirts. Of course, I have no choice but to jostle people and most in the bar are cool with that. Most — but not all.

Two guys turn and glare at me as I brush past one of them, slightly knocking him and causing a miniscule amount of lager to spill from his pint. They've got to be about 18 years old at most. 'You spilt my pint man,' says the bigger one, affecting what he clearly thinks is a threatening look. 'Yeah, sorry mate, it's just a bit crowded tonight. Enjoy the game,' I say as I turn to move away. 'He wants to know what you're gonna do about it,' whines the smaller one, half-hiding, half-smiling and laughing nervously — he reminds me of one of those hyenas you see on the Discovery channel. I feel my heckles start to rise and I turn back round to face them. 'Well, why doesn't he ask me then?' I say, squaring off. There's a heartbeat where they falter but then they get brave again. The pint in question obviously isn't their first tonight. 'You better watch it mate, I've done Karate,' says the bigger one. The smaller one licks his lips in anticipation. It's time to end this.

'Well, that's different, mate,' I say, handing him my untouched pint. 'Why didn't you say so?'

I smile as I head for the door. I wish when I'd been a cocky, drunk kid, I'd have been lucky enough to pick on me...

FORMALITES

Shugo	Line up
Kio tsuke	Attention
Rei	Bow
Onegai shimasu	Please teach me
Shomen ni rei	Bow to the front
Seiza	Kneel
Mokuso	Meditation
Yame	Stop
Kiritsu	Stand
Yasuma	Rest (stand easy)
Otagai ni rei	Bow to each other
Sensei ni rei	Bow to the teacher
Domo arigato gozaimashita	Thank you

COUNTING

Ichi	One
Ni	Two
San	Three
Shi	Four
Go	Five
Roku	Six
Shichi	Seven
Hachi	Eight
Ku	Nine
Ju	Ten

GENERAL TERMINOLOGY

Kyoshi	Teacher of teachers
Shihan	Master
Sensei	Teacher
Sempai	Senior student
Dojo	Training area
Gi	Training suit
Obi	Belt
Hai	Yes
Kiai	Spirit shout
Rei	Bow
Yoi	Ready
Kamae	On guard
Hajime	Start
Yame	Stop
Mae	Front
Ushiro	Back
Yoko	Side
Mawate	Turn
Kata	Forms

GENERAL TERMINOLOGY (CONTINUED)

Kumite	Sparring
Kihon	Basics
Bunkai	Analysis / application
Muchimi	Heavy / sticky
Tai sabaki	Body movement
Suri ashi	Sliding step
Sukami hike	Grab and pull

AREAS OF THE BODY

Jodan	Upper level
Chudan	Middle level
Gedan	Lower level
Seiken	Fist
Empi	Elbow
Hiza	Knee
Shuto	Knife hand
Haito	Ridge hand
Taisho	Palm heel
Kakato	Heel
Maisoku	Top of foot
Sokuto	Edge of foot
Koshi	Ball of foot
Kogan	Groin
Ken	Knuckle
Ude	Forearm

STANCES — DACHI

Heisoku dachi	Attention / feet together
Musubi dachi	Attention / feet splayed
Heiko dachi	Feet parallel and apart
Sanchin dachi	Hour-glass stance
Zenkutsu dachi	Forward stance
Kiba dachi	Horse riding stance
Shiko dachi	Box stance
Neko ashi dachi	Cat stance
Kokutsu dachi	Long cat stance
Sagi ashi dachi	Crane stance
Hankutsu dachi	Short zenkutsu
Naname	Angled (45 degrees)

PUNCHES — TSUKI

Gyaku tsuki	Reverse
Oi tsuki	Lunge
Kizami tsuki	Jab
Kagi tsuki	Hook

PUNCHES — TSUKI (CONTINUED)

Kosa tsuki	Cross
Jun tsuki	Same side
Age tsuki	Upper-cut
Awase tsuki	Double punch
Ippon ken	Single knuckle
Nakadaka ken	Middle knuckle

KICKS — GERI

Mae geri	Front
Mawashi geri	Roundhouse
Yoko geri	Side
Kansetsu geri	Knee joint
Kogan geri	Groin
Mata geri	Thigh
Ushiro geri	Back
Kakato geri	Heel kick
Fumikomi geri	Stamp
Naname fumikomi geri	Inner stamp
Tobi geri	Jumping

TECHNIQUES — WAZA

Nage waza	Throwing techniques
Ne waza	Ground fighting techniques
Shime waza	Strangulation and choking techniques
Kansetsu waza	Joint locking and breaking techniques
Atemi waza	Vital point striking techniques

BLOCKS — UKE

Jodan age uke	Upper block
Chudan uke	Middle block
Gedan barai	Lower sweep
Kake uke	Hook block
Hike uke	Wrist roll block
Soto uke	Inward block
Mawashi uke	Wheelhouse block
Shuto uke	Knife hand block
Ko uke	Crane's head block
Ura uke	Top of hand block
Jogi uke	One up one down
Juji uke	X block
Soe uke	Assisted block

BLOCKS — UKE (CONTINUED)

Sukui uke	Scoop block
Osae uke	Pressing block

STRIKES — UCHI

Hiza	Knee
Taisho	Palm heel
Nukite	Spearhand
Uraken	Backfist
Shikyo	Throat grab
Empi	Elbow
Haito	Ridge hand
Tetsui	Hammerfist
Shuto	Knifehand
Kaiko	Chisel fist
Zutsuki	Head-butt
Hitokui	Biting
Teketsu	Gouging

THROWS — NAGE WAZA

Ashi barai	Foot sweep
Osoto gari	Outer leg reap
Tai otoshi	Body drop
O goshi	Major hip
Harai goshi	Sweeping hip
Ippon seoinage	Single shoulder
Morote seoinage	Double shoulder
Uchi mata	Inner thigh
Tomoe nage	Stomach throw
Kata guruma	Shoulder wheel

GROUND FIGHTING — NE WAZA

Randori	Free practice
Soko shihai	Guard
Yoko shihai	Side control
Kami shihai	Mount
Hadaka jime	Naked strangle
Kosa jime	Cross strangle
Okuri-eri jime	Lapel strangle
Sangaku jime	Triangle choke
Juji gatame	Cross leg arm bar
Ude garami	Figure 4 arm lock
Gyaku ude garami	Reverse figure 4

ACKNOW LEDGEMENTS

Acknowledgements

Over the process of converting *Four Shades of Black* from an idea into a physical reality, two things have stood out which both surprised and humbled me. The first was the sheer amount of help that I needed to bring the book to fruition; the second was how freely that help was given.

First and foremost I would like to dedicate this book to my father, George Mulholland, whose boundless energy, open mind, and deep love of the martial arts set me firmly on the path of discovery that I still follow today.

Secondly, I need to express my gratitude to my teachers. While the thoughts, arguments, and conclusions in this book do not necessarily reflect their views, these men have nevertheless had a fundamental effect on my understanding of the martial arts, on me as a martial artist, and on me as a person.

Kim Roberts for teaching and shaping me. Steve Morris for helping me to understand. Nick Hughes for the deep-rooted street-wise practicality. It has truly been a privilege.

Cliché though it may be, this book would genuinely never have been written without the constant pressure/encouragement of my student and friend, Goran Powell. A gentle yet relentless force really can move mountains. Thank you.

I also owe a great debt of gratitude to Iain Abernethy and Geoff Thompson for their advice, encouragement and support – all freely given without debt or judgement simply because I asked for help. True martial artists both.

The book looks the way it does because of the skills, professionalism and kindness of art director and designer Adrian Nitsch, artworker Ben Hung, photographer Richard Pullar and production manager Elese Fisher.

To those students who gave up their time for the photo shoot: Goran Powell, Akintunde Oladimeji, Dominic Du Plooy, Sonja Klug and Cassandra Backus. To Dan Lewis, Alan Vokes and to the great many others who have taught me, trained with me, or trained under me. I have learned from you all and I am grateful for all that you have given.

Finally, I would like to thank my wife, Genevieve, and my children, Tiger and Isis, for their love, patience, and support. My art takes me away from them far more than I would like and the sacrifices of the martial arts are not mine alone.

My deep and sincere thanks to you all.

About the Author

Gavin Mulholland
5th Dan Okinawan Goju Ryu
Chief Instructor Daigaku Karate Kai London

Gavin began training alongside his brothers at an early age with his father, who taught Judo and unarmed combat in the British Forces in Northern Ireland in the 1960s. On moving to the South of England in the 1970s, he began training in Goju Ryu Karate under Goju master Kyoshi Kim Roberts.

In over 30 years of training, Gavin has travelled extensively throughout Asia, training in Thailand, Indonesia, China and Japan.

Gavin has 15 years' experience working on the doors of pubs and clubs around the UK; was a regular instructor for one of the UK's leading bodyguard, close protection and door supervisor security groups; and is a former lecturer in psychology for two London universities.

His association, Daigaku Karate Kai (DKK) is one of the UK's leading Goju Ryu associations with dojos in London and Bristol. While firmly advocating and promoting traditional training methods as outlined in this book, DKK have competed successfully in cage fighting events, most notably Cage Rage, the UK's foremost MMA organisation.

Gavin has made numerous TV and film appearances, is a widely published author within the martial arts community, and was inaugurated into The Combat Hall of Fame in 2002.

For further insight into Daigaku Karate Kai visit
www.goju-karate.co.uk

*"Luckily, there are people like Gavin still out there proving
that Traditional Martial Arts do indeed work"*

Nick Hughes \ Chief Instructor of Fight Survival Training
(F.I.S.T.) and Combat Karate

*"Gavin embodies all that is good and worthwhile in the arts.
I cannot recommend his teaching highly enough"*

David Rubens \ 5th Dan Yoshinkan Aikido